99

Obama
Blogs

By
Will Clark

99
Obama
Blogs

Copyright© 2014 by Will Clark

ISBN 13: 9781500590840
ISBN 10: 1500590843

Published by
Motivation Basics
P.O. Box 6327
Diamondhead, MS 39525
Will01@aol.com

For more information about the author
visit

http://www.authorsden.com/visit/author.asp?authorid=1496

Contents

QUOTE

"A nation can survive its fools, and even the ambitious. But it cannot survive treason from within. An enemy at the gates is less formidable, for he is known and carries his banner openly. But the traitor moves amongst those within the gate freely, his sly whispers rustling through all the alleys, heard in the very halls of government itself. For the traitor appears not a traitor; he speaks in accents familiar to his victims, and he wears their face and their arguments, he appeals to the baseness that lies deep in the hearts of all men. He rots the soul of a nation, he works secretly and unknown in the night to undermine the pillars of the city, he infects the body politic so that it can no longer resist. A murderer is less to fear. The traitor is the plague." *Marcus Tullius Cicero, 58 B.C. Speech in the Roman Senate*

INTRODUCTION

Barack Hussein Obama began his presidential campaign with a promise to 'share the wealth' of the country and to 'spread the wealth around.' He never once promised to create an environment in America to help the poor earn their share of the wealth. His was a promise to give them something, not to give them the opportunity to earn something for themselves by being part of productive society. He promised the poor a free dole.

His initial action was to create class warfare by separating the consciousness of American society. He labeled their enemy as the 'millionaires and billionaires' so their target would have a classification and could be identified. He would be their savior to make those millionaires and billionaires share their wealth with them. They believed him and they followed him. Many even worshiped him as a deity. They became his 'doles.' His doles will follow anywhere he leads them, even into places alien to the visions of our Founding Fathers.

Obama has used the same practices and techniques as did Vladimir Lenin in Russia and Adolph Hitler in Germany to create loyal followers. He told his doles what they wanted to hear - and he became powerful. Lenin convinced the proletariat, George Orwell's proles, the ruling class was their enemy. His proles helped him destroy a once proud Russia. Jewish merchants were Hitler's target. He convinced poor Germans they were keeping Germans from being successful, and they followed Hitler to destroy Germany's once great nation.

The blogs in this writing are taken from those I posted on my site at Authorsden during the past two years. Blogs I wrote prior to that time were published in another book titled: '101 Obama Blogs' which is also available in print. In combination, they reveal my belief that Barack Obama is a danger to the survival of our great country, the United States of America, similar to the danger created by Lenin and Hitler. His, however, is more insidious and cunning.

These blogs are posted on my blog site at Authorsden.com. They are numbered and arranged in no particular order, only as published at that site. There are many more blogs posted at that site.

99 Blogs

**About
Barack Obama
and His
Administration**

**Posted on my
Blog Site**

**Authorsden.com
During Years
2013-2014**

1

Old Racist White Men

This is a quote I place on the first page of all my political books concerning our current government - the government of Barack Obama. Perhaps it's just an historical footnote - or perhaps it's a warning for any moment in time. Perhaps only time will tell - when our current moment is history.

QUOTE:

"A nation can survive its fools, and even the ambitious. But it cannot survive treason from within. An enemy at the gates is less formidable, for he is known and carries his banner openly. But the traitor moves amongst those within the gate freely, his sly whispers rustling through all the alleys, heard in the very halls of government itself. For the traitor appears not a traitor; he speaks in accents familiar to his victims, and he wears their face and their arguments, he appeals to the baseness that lies deep in the hearts of all men. He rots the soul of a nation, he works secretly and unknown in the night to undermine the pillars of the city, he infects the body politic so that it can no longer resist. A murderer is less to fear. The traitor is the plague." *Marcus Tullius Cicero, 58 B.C. Speech in the Roman Senate. End of Quote.*

Some of you might remember that as a result of Obama's re-election in 2012, I wrote a book titled, 'The Day America Died.' Since then, five reviews have been posted for that book. One was a 5-star, one a 4-star, and three are 1-star. There's a common thread to those 1-stars. This extract from one of those is a perfect example:

"This book simply recites the same tired old talking points that the people who formerly controlled this country use to excuse and cover up their racism and fear about a new dawning in human affairs. They are losing their minds now that the old idea of America as a multi-cultural melting pot is actually coming true. They have to deny fact that President Obama is a far better president than GWB ever was in order to reaffirm their belief that his presidency is just an anomaly and not the dawning of a new day."

This negative comment is typical of all the others. The common thread is that there are no facts to dispute my writings and no argument on a positive side to detail Obama's 'achievements.' They are simply attacks against the writer and those who share those beliefs. Another 1-star rating stated those who disagree with Obama's actions are a bunch of "old racist white men." Not one negative rater gave one single achievement by Obama.

Now, consider some facts that make us 'old racist white men' suspicious of Obama's activities:

1. Iranian and other radical Islamist terrorists have been training in Argentina and Brazil.

2. Obama released five radical Islamist leaders from incarceration to return to their activities.

3. Obama is drawing down and weakening those who protect us - our military.

4. Border Patrol agents are now overwhelmed by the massive flow Obama created.

5. Harry Reid just proclaimed, "Our border is secure!"

Do these activities by Obama not create questions by those other than 'old racist white men?' Perhaps we should all take that quote above very seriously - even those who believe Obama is their god. Perhaps only history will judge.

God bless America.

2
Who are the Terrorists?

In Jan 2011, I released a novel titled: 'America 20XX: The New World Order.' Although it was 'fiction,' in that book I described how Islamic terrorists were slipping across our southern borders to pre-position until a designated time. That book had a momentary positive ending. The major question today is; will the current reality on our southern borders also have a positive ending for patriotic Americans?

Current events allowed - or arranged - by Obama's administration suggest not. Are more terrorists allowed to rush across our borders from the chaos created by Obama's border policies? This link clearly answers that question:

http://toprightnews.com/?p=1613

This poses another question regarding guns. Many people, especially those most loyal to Obama, believe in strict gun control - or the elimination of private ownership of weapons. Now here's the revealing and important question: if you lived in a border state and late one night you heard noises outside your door - or loud banging on your door - how would you feel if your wife and children looked at you and said, "protect us?" Would you tell them you would call 911 and everything would be okay - the police would be there as soon as they could?"

Those of us who are not deceived by Obama believe otherwise. We believe we have not only a right, but also a duty to defend ourselves and our loved ones - and America. If terrorists, and others, knew that every American family was armed it's likely they wouldn't be so bold. Perhaps loyal and dutiful citizens would never have to fire a single shot. But, what about those bullets?

Possibly, Obama is attempting back door gun control by hoarding all the important bullets America produces. Many ammunition shortages now exist. What could happen from that action? Sporting store mangers told me that Russia would provide bullets if they become unavailable through normal sources. Would Obama declare people who buy ammunition on the black market from Russia as 'terrorists?' What would happen then - who would Obama claim are the real terrorists? Would Obama's new-generation civilian army fire on these citizen terrorists?

God bless America.

3

Who is the Enemy?

What battle is Barack Obama arming to fight? His administration keeps ordering and buying more bullets - many of them hollow-points. This is some information I extracted from several articles to examine that question:

A little more than a year ago, the Social Security Administration put in a request for 174,000 rounds of ".357 Sig 125 grain bonded jacketed hollow-point" bullets.

Before that, it was the Department of Agriculture requesting 320,000 rounds. More recently, the Department of Homeland Security raised eyebrows with its request for 450 million rounds — at about the same time the FBI separately sought 100 million hollow-point rounds.

The National Oceanic and Atmospheric Administration also requested 46,000 rounds. Philip Van Cleave, president of the Virginia Citizens Defense League, asked: why exactly does a weather service need ammunition? "NOAA — really? They have a need? One just doesn't know why they're doing this," he said. "The problem is, all these agencies have their own SWAT teams, their own police departments, which is crazy. In theory, it was supposed to be the U.S. marshals that was the armed branch for the federal government."

Brian Koenig, writing for The New American, put the DHS purchase in perspective: To put the 1.6 billion rounds in ammunition — which, note, the agency purchased in the last 10 months — in perspective, during the peak of active battle operations in Iraq, U.S. armed forces used approximately 5.5 million bullets a month. "Extrapolating the figures," InfoWars.com reports, "the DHS has purchased enough bullets over the last 10 months to wage a full scale war for almost 30 years."

In late 2012, the Social Security Administration posted a purchasing request for 174,000 rounds of .357 125 grain bonded jacketed hollow point bullets. The Department of Agriculture (USDA) began seeking 320,000 rounds of ammo around the same time. The National Oceanic Atmospheric Administration (NOAA) also posted a notice seeking 46,000 rounds of ammunition.

WND.com, Joseph Farah, wrote on 2-3-2013 "Is the U.S. government getting ready for a war we don't know about? And, if that's why Washington is stockpiling massive amounts of ammunition (hollow points, by the way), why is Homeland Security doing the buying instead of the Defense Department? We've learned more about Obama's vision since then. Maybe it's time for a review:

He made the campaign promise to build this $439 billion domestic army, but all references to the initiative were inexplicably deleted from the copy of his speech posted on his website while others mysteriously disappeared from transcripts of the speech distributed by the campaign. That was strange – and ominous."

Do you remember presidential candidate Barack Obama's little-noticed announcement that, if elected in 2008, he wanted to create a "civilian national security force" as big, as strong and as well-funded as the Defense Department?

From Whiteout Press: It seems the conclusion of our Whiteout Press investigation is that while there may be a conspiracy, it's no theory - the US federal government is purchasing and hoarding large quantities of small arms ammunition. And the fact that dozens of agencies that have no reason to be heavily armed are arming themselves to the teeth, and the fact that agencies like DHS are contradicting their own numbers, both lend credence to the fears that something unusual is going on. What that 'something' might be remains to be seen.

Why does Barack Obama seem unconcerned and disinterested in the chaos going on at our southern borders? When that chaos gets worse and more out of control will that be his cue to announce an emergency - and declare martial law? How did he know that would happen? Why has he pre-positioned so much ammunition - so much deadly and lethal ammunition? Who is it targeted to be used against? His activities and comments have been totally smug recently. Does he know something he's not telling us? Are we in danger, soon, of losing our American freedoms - how soon?

God bless America.

4

Is Our Southern Border the Beginning?

Adolph Hitler blamed the Jews for Germany's problems - and he created a riot group of 'Brown Shirts' to harass and intimidate them. Later, six million Jews were slaughtered by his followers. At that time, Hitler, with only a small dedicated group, created havoc and destruction throughout the world. Only a nation founded on Christian principles could stop him: the United States of America. Many of our brave soldiers prayed to God when they knew they were about to die for that cause - freedom. Many times God was their only support as they cringed alone in their foxholes or dashed across open areas filled with machine gun fire. What hope would they have had without God beside them?

Will Republicans and Christians become Obama's 'Jews' in the future? Clearly Obama has created, encouraged, or allowed a major crisis on our southern borders. Why? Some think it's to create a massive surge in new Democrat voters as they age. This could be the valid reason, but perhaps not. What if Obama does not have time for that to evolve - to fulfill his real goal; the goal of being our unchallenged totalitarian leader? At this point - does he care about votes?

Could confusion and chaos on the border, perhaps eventually mixed with terrorist acts, be Obama's excuse to proclaim martial law, and to suspend free rights of American citizens? He consistently blames Republicans for lack of legislation - the legislation HE wants - and uses that as an excuse for his increasing executive actions, too many times violating our Constitution and creating more chaos. All the while he continues to accuse Republicans as being the source of the border problem - and all other problems in our nation; eerily similar to the charge Hitler made against the Jews.

Also, similar to Hitler, he has his tight group of supporters encouraging and protecting him, and defending his actions. Confusion on the border allows many options for Obama; which many patriotic citizens might support to eliminate the crisis - maybe even accepting the idea that the confusion is so great martial law is the only appropriate option. Once in total control, would he ever let go?

What are Obama's real intentions? When will those intentions be known?

God bless America.

5

The Growing War Against Christians

I recently wrote a long article about the growing war against Christians in the United States. This current article excerpt is another clear example of that war:

"Senate Majority Leader Harry Reid said Monday that Democrats will take up legislation in the "coming weeks" to address last month's Supreme Court decision that allowed some employers with religious objections to opt out of Obamacare's contraception mandate.

Democrats on Capitol Hill have overwhelmingly criticized the high court's ruling in the Hobby Lobby case and are working to craft a response that would restore the coverage, though no specifics have yet been outlined.

"We're going to do something about the Hobby Lobby legislation," Reid said on the Senate floor Monday as he ticked off the Senate's to-do list over the next several weeks." End of excerpt.

You might ask how this is an example of the 'war against Christians?' The answer is simple: Hobby Lobby is not objecting to providing 'contraception.' Their insurance plan covers that provision; the Democrats are not telling you that. Hobby Lobby is objecting to promoting 'abortion.'

Many people, especially Christians, believe abortion is the same as murder - the killing of a person. If Hobby Lobby believes abortion is the same as murder, should they be required to participate in murder? Is that any different than killing an alone, homeless, and useless person on the streets? What purpose does that person serve in the grand scheme of life? Perhaps the answer to that question involves consideration of another question: what is the 'soul?'

Of course, no mortal really knows what a soul is; and I certainly wouldn't suggest I know or understand. However, there are some modern ideas and discoveries that offer at least little tidbits of theory. Let's consider electricity, cells, and energy molecules we know are there but don't understand their sources.

So, what about electricity - or something comparable to or similar to electricity? We can't see electricity; does that mean it doesn't exist? What if God is not an old white-haired man often personified in art; what if God is not human-like at all? Does that mean He could not exist in form such as electricity? According to scripture, Jesus was sent in human form as God's visible representative. If electricity were connected throughout the universe, and it all led back to one central source, could that not create a divine connection between God and humanity? Would that source not last forever and ever?

We can also consider human cells. Human cells don't just hang around in our bodies as fat little blobs killing time. Each of the billions of them has a purpose, and they are given energy to fulfill their purpose. What if one of those cells, or invisible energy sources, hidden somewhere in our body was the 'life' cell, the one planted at conception to make the attachment to God and His universe. Do all cells and all energy have to die when one dies? Have you ever heard of spores? Some live forever. Is it inconceivable that a single cell could hold the hereafter energy until time for resurrection? Is it not possible that that small amount of space and energy could hold all our thoughts of the past and our expectations of the future back to our original source? Is it not possible that when the 'Book of Life' is opened for judgment, we are not there opening ourselves to judge ourselves?

Perhaps Heaven is that re-connection to the God source to live forever and ever. Perhaps Hell is the realization one judges himself or herself that he or she rejected that eternal connection during his or her lifetime, and therefore that self-judgment never got instilled into the 'forever' cell. Perhaps that invisible energy source flows through the universe forever with the lasting sense of not recognizing or respecting its original source. Perhaps Hell is nowhere and nonexistence and is the antithesis of awareness of belonging to the eternal life source. Perhaps. Perhaps only God knows.

Perhaps the people at Hobby Lobby and other Christians believe that when human life is destroyed, even as a fetus, that is also a destruction of God's plan for the expanding universe of life. Perhaps that soul isn't given an opportunity, and its full time, to reach out and find its purpose in the universe.

The war against God and Christians grows stronger in the United States. But, it's no surprise to Christians who can read. It's written. When and how will it end?

God bless America.

6

What are His Real Plans for America?

Do you remember Obama's comment during a campaign stop in Colorado on July 2, 2008: "We cannot continue to rely only on our military in order to achieve the national security objectives we've set. We've got to have a civilian national security force that's just as powerful, just as strong, just as well-funded." It seems Obama is still focused on that plan to arm America for some 'internal' national security threat, as he draws down our military to defend against an external security threat. What are his "national security objectives" we've set?

This article by Kit Daniels at Infowars.com, February 5, 2014 gives more current information:

"Post Office joins other federal agencies stockpiling over two billion rounds of ammo:"

UPDATE: Since the publication of this article, the USPS has amended its pre-solicitation, claiming that the ammunition is a "standard purchase" for the Postal Police. This does not explain, however, why the Postal Police was not listed in the original notice if this is standard. As the federal government grows larger, more and more federal agencies such as the Dept. of Education and NOAA are forming and arming their own "law enforcement divisions" with hundreds of thousands spent on full-blown arsenals. Even the EPA has its own SWAT teams conducting raids on peaceful Americans. Expect to see more large-scale firearm and ammunition purchases by these bureaucracies as they become even more militarized.

The U.S. Postal Service joins the long list of non-military federal agencies purchasing large amounts of ammunition. On Jan. 31, the USPS Supplies and Services Purchasing Office posted a notice on the Federal Business Opportunities website asking contractors to register with USPS as potential ammunition suppliers for a variety of cartridges. "The United States Postal Service intends to solicit proposals for assorted small arms ammunition," the notice reads, which also mentioned a deadline of Feb. 10.

Ironically the Postal Service isn't the first non-law enforcement agency seeking firearms and ammunition. Since 2001, the U.S. Dept. of Education has been building a massive arsenal through purchases orchestrated by the Bureau of Alcohol, Tobacco and Firearms. The Education Dept. has spent over $80,000 so far on Glock pistols and over $17,000 on Remington shotguns.

Back in July, the National Oceanic and Atmospheric Administration also purchased 72,000 rounds of .40 Smith & Wesson, following a 2012 purchase for 46,000 rounds of .40 S&W jacketed hollow point by the National Weather Service. NOAA spokesperson Scott Smullen responded to concerns over the weather service purchase by stating that it was meant for the NOAA Fisheries Office of Law Enforcement for its bi-annual "target qualifications and training."

That seems excessive considering that JHP ammunition is typically several times more expensive than practice rounds, which can usually be found in equivalent power loadings and thus offer similar recoil characteristics as duty rounds.

Including mass purchases by the Dept. of Homeland Security, non-military federal agencies combined have purchased an estimated amount of over two billion rounds of ammunition in the past two years.

Additionally, the U.S. Army bought almost 600,000 Soviet AK-47 magazines last fall, enough to hold nearly 18,000,000 rounds of 7.62x39mm ammo which is not standard-issue for either the U.S. military or even NATO. It would take a Lockheed Martin C-5 Galaxy, one of the largest cargo aircraft in the world, two trips to haul that many magazines.

A month prior, the army purchased nearly 3,000,000 rounds of 7.62x39mm ammo, a huge amount but still only 1/6th of what the magazines purchased can hold in total.

The Feds have also spent millions on riot control measures in addition to the ammo acquisitions.

Earlier this month, Homeland Security spent over $58 million on hiring security details for just two Social Security offices in Maryland.

DHS also spent $80 million on armed guards to protect government buildings in New York and sought even more guards for federal facilities in Wisconsin and Minnesota.

While the government gears up for civil unrest and stockpiles ammo without limit, private gun owners on the other hand are finding ammunition shelves empty at gun stores across America, including shortages of once-common cartridges such as .22 Long Rifle." End of Article.

Perhaps Obama's 'civilian national security force is on the way. What is its purpose? Does the crisis and chaos on our southern border have any connection to that armed security force? Would Obama's army fire on innocent American citizens if they were proclaimed 'terrorists' trying to protect our nation? Would this not be a perfect time to declare 'martial law' to gain total control over a once free nation?

Two historical incidents detailed in my new book, 'Denied 3 Times' suggest armed government civilian forces will fire upon innocent American citizens if ordered to do so. They are the incidents at Ruby Ridge and David Koresh and the Branch Dividians. Women and children were also killed in these incidents.

What does Obama plan for America? Why does he need this much ammunition and armaments?

God bless America.

7

More War Against Christians

I just finished my final edit for my new book, 'Denied 3 Times,' and submitted it back to the print publisher for the final proof; which if all goes well I will review online and mark, 'approved' in only a few hours from now. The book is free online in digital format at Smashwords

When I began the book, I didn't know where I was going with it. At first, I just wanted to show the historical significance between Peter's three denials of Jesus when the Romans came to arrest him, and the three denials of Jesus at the 2012 Democratic National Convention. As I watched that take place at the convention, I knew it was an important and prophetic event. Why were there three votes and three denials at that convention? What were the odds of there being three votes - all denying placing the name of God in the party's platform? I didn't know where the book would take me, but as I typed it found its own way. The result was a book about the war on God, Christianity, and Christians. Until I began researching I didn't realize this war was so deep and deadly worldwide, including the United States - and prophetic.

Chapter 1 (10 pages) describes many of Barack Obama's actions against God and Christianity. Chapter 2 (18 pages) cites specific examples of the war against Christians. Chapter 3 (16 pages) cites more specific examples of actions against Christians - including many deaths. Chapter 4 (24 pages) cites many activities of 'America's Most Biblically-Hostile President.' Chapter 5 (21 pages) is titled: 'Why the Hatred for Christianity.'

While I was in the final edit, I was also listening to news - especially reports about the Hobby Lobby decision. The conclusion is generally that Democrats will use that decision to claim that Republicans are continuing their 'war on women.' Of course, this conclusion is debatable depending upon whether you are a Democrat or a Republican. While I was editing and listening an idea came to mind for the Republicans to counter the Democratic claim that they are making war against women.

My research indicates that most war against God and Christians in the United States is perpetuated by Democrats. It would be as valid for the Republicans to claim that Democrats have a war against God, as it is for Democrats to claim that Republicans have a war against women. I wonder if Republicans have as much guts to do that as the Democrats have to continue their claim. Or, should the Republicans just stand there and do nothing but try to defend themselves against those claims by Democrats? I don't know of any defensive wars that have ever been won.

God bless America.

8

More Emphasis on Obama

Very interesting. It's very interesting what book sales can suggest or indicate. I have a fairly large number of books listed here at AD. And, they cover a wide rage of topics and genres. I am fully cognizant that an author should remain dedicated mostly to one genre to develop a following and a reputation in that genre - especially at my age; 75. However, realizing that I likely will never sell enough books to make writing my main income source, I write mostly about what's on my mind at any given time; from novels, to non-fiction success books, to children's books, to politics and current events.

In my political books I try to express my sincere concern for the future of our great nation. Even in my latest novels, I try to include the implications of current political events. At the moment that's my greatest concern. With this wide range, I still don't sell many books, maybe 12 to 20 a month. However, even with that small number I have observed a trend lately.

In the past, my sales have been wide-spread suggesting no marketing strategy that I could latch onto and explore. Recently however, especially this month, it seems a trend is developing. Most of my sales this month, although few, seem to be more inquisitiveness about Barack Obama. Most of my sales are digital. This month, most of those sales have been: Obama's Ring: The Seat of Satan and King Obama: America's Greatest Danger. The only three non-digital books I just sold are: Obama's World: Secrets and Deceptions.

This trend seems to indicate that more people are beginning to question the qualifications, motivations, and intentions of this man I perceive as being a great danger to our nation - Barack Obama. Perhaps this new sales trend suggests a little spark of hope that our great nation might survive. Anyway, a little optimism is better than none.

God bless America.

9

Final Thought

Islamists are determined to destroy Western civilization. It's the total focus of their planned destiny; it's all they focus on and dream of. It's in their thoughts, their writings, and their strategies. They are not subtle about that mission. They throw it in our faces and dare us to resist. It seems they want us to resist for an excuse to kill - behead - more human beings.

To proceed openly and full-speed ahead, they must first remove the 'one that restrains.' Some people believe this relates to the time of the 'Rapture' when all Christian believers will suddenly and miraculously be taken to Heaven - and will just disappear from the face of the earth and rule with Christ for the Millennium, that thousand years. This is not the case at all.

First, the word or the idea of a Rapture does not exist in the Bible. Second, only the souls of those beheaded for not denying their Christian faith, and refusing the mark of the beast during this period, will occupy that Millennial position as explained in Revelation 20:4-6. This is identified as the 'first resurrection.' The 'second resurrection' includes all others as explained in 20:12-13. This is where the other souls are judged from the 'book of life - according to their works.'

The 'one that restrains,' at this point, seems to be the power of the United States. To accomplish their mission, America must be subdued - restrained.

Many American citizens, and other Westerners, are now training with the Sunni (terrorist) invasion in Iraq, which includes portions of Iraq and Syria. Will these citizens later begin terrorist attacks in America to create a condition of fear that will allow Obama to claim a national emergency and martial law, and refuse to step down as president at the time stipulated in our Constitution? Perhaps the Iranian threat of a nuclear attack, and the importance of their Shiite Mahdi, will be another factor supporting Obama's claim of a national emergency. If this happens will this be the end of humanity and freedom as we understand it in human and religious terms?

What might be the first significant signs to warn of that coming event? First, more confusion and terrorist attacks might occur on our southern borders - while our distracted focus is on guarding New York. Second, many Christians could be targeted as terrorists - or as supporters of terrorism. Finally, cash transactions will be eliminated under the guise of fighting terrorism. When that happens, everyone must make the choice to accept or not accept the mark of the beast so they can buy and sell - just to survive. It will be an important time and a serious choice for Christians. Will Christians who refuse to comply be branded as 'terrorists?'

More is explained in my new book: 'Denied 3 Times.' It's now available FREE at Smashwords.

God bless America.

10

Saul Alinsky

I got this information in an email, but forgot the origin. The sender asked recipients to 'pass it on.' I edited it slightly for size, but this blog is fundamentally the same. It concerns the influence of Saul Alinsky on our current politics:

Saul Alinsky died about 43 years ago, but his writings continue to influence many in political control of our nation today. Hillary did her college thesis on his writings and Obama writes about him in his books.

Alinsky's important books are: 'Rules for Radicals' and 'Reveille for Radicals.' In the books he explains how to create a social state. According to him there are eight levels of control that must be obtained before you are able to create a social state. The first is the most important.

1) Healthcare– Control healthcare and you control the people.

2) Poverty – Increase the poverty level as high as possible, poor people are easier to control and will not fight back if you are providing everything for them to live.

3) Debt – Increase the debt to an unsustainable level. That way you are able to increase taxes, and this will produce more poverty.

4) Gun Control– Remove the ability to defend themselves from the government. That way you are able to create a police state.

5) Welfare – Take control of every aspect of their lives (Food, Housing, and Income.)

6) Education – Take control of what people read and listen to – take control of what children learn in school.

7) Religion – Remove the belief in the God from the Government and schools.

8) Class Warfare – Divide the people into the wealthy and the poor. This will cause more discontent and it will be easier to take (Tax) the wealthy with the support of the poor.

Alinsky merely simplified Vladimir Lenin's original scheme for world conquest by communism, under Russian rule. Stalin described his converts as "Useful Idiots." The Useful Idiots have destroyed every nation in which they have seized power and control. It is presently happening at an alarming rate in the U.S. According to Alinsky: "It is difficult to free fools from the chains they revere."

I had never heard that term before, "Useful Idiots," so I went to Wikipedia. This is part of the Wikipedia description:

"In political jargon, useful idiot is a term for people perceived as propagandists for a cause whose goals they are not fully aware of, and who are used cynically by the leaders of the cause.

Despite often being attributed to Lenin, in 1987, Grant Harris, senior reference librarian at the Library of Congress, declared that "We have not been able to identify this phrase among [Lenin's] published works."

In Russian language, the equivalent term "useful fools" was in use at least in 1941.

A similar term, useful innocents, appears in Austrian-American economist Ludwig von Mises's "Planned Chaos" (1947). Von Mises claims the term was used by communists for liberals that von Mises describes as "confused and misguided sympathizers". The term useful innocents also appears in a Readers Digest article (1946) titled "Yugoslavia's Tragic Lesson to the World", an excerpt from a, at the time, forthcoming book (no title printed) authored by Bogdan Raditsa (Bogdan Radica), a "high ranking official of the Yugoslav Government". Raditsa says: "In the Serbo-Croat language the communists have a phrase for true democrats who consent to collaborate with them for 'democracy.' It is Korisne Budale, or Useful Innocents." Although Raditsa translates the phrase as "Useful Innocents", the word budala (plural: budale) actually translates as "fool" and synonyms thereof."

Interesting. Do any of the eight rules and the terms listed above seem connected to current events here in America?

God bless America.

11

Fleeing to the Wilderness

In the past, nearly all Americans worshiped God and gave thanks for the creation of our country and for its great blessings. Through Obama's leadership and influence God's name now has been cast out and unwelcome from many institutions in America. How far will these exclusions go; perhaps to the point of total exclusions and even persecution? Does not evil and persecution left unchecked become more acceptable and normal; does it not often lead to tyranny? How can evil be recognized and judged in a society not influenced by respect for God's creation? Will Obama's influence create a condition that one day might cause Christians and Jews to flee to the wilderness? Perhaps this war on Christians is foretold in Revelations, Chapter 12. Pertinent verses in the chapter include:

"And there appeared a great wonder in heaven; a woman clothed with the sun, and the moon under her feet, and upon her head a crown of twelve stars." (Have you ever heard of the twelve tribes of Israel?)

Verse 2: "And she being with child cried, travailing in birth, and pained to be delivered." (Wasn't there much persecution of believers in the beginning of Christianity?)

Verse 4: "--- and the dragon stood before the woman which was ready to be delivered, for to devour her child as soon as it was born."(Remember the 'slaughter of the innocents? The Devil is always lurking to destroy those who believe in Jesus.)

Verse 5: "And she brought forth a man child, who was to rule all nations with a rod of iron; and her child was caught up unto God, and to his throne."

Verse 6: and the woman fled into the wilderness, where she hath a place prepared of God, that they should feed her there for a thousand two hundred and threescore days." (The abomination of desolation - when the place of God in Jerusalem will be occupied by the beast and his forces. Jews (and Christians) are warned to flee. Many believe this place of God will be the rebuilt temple.)

Verse 17: "And the dragon was wroth with the woman, and went to make war with the remnant of her seed, which keep the commandments of God, and have the testimony of Jesus Christ."(Does this not describe the present day war on Christianity? The mention of God and Jesus in many public places, especially government places, is becoming less tolerated even here in America.)

Although John wrote Revelation, the Apocalypse, two thousand years ago while exiled on the Island of Patmos by Emporer Domitian many of his written visions seem more relevant today than in the past. History, events, and communications seem destined to explain his visions more every day. One merely has to look, read, and listen with an open and objective spirit.

Judeo-Christians are now being persecuted and belittled even more throughout the world since Obama became president. The world has become even more dangerous since his re-election in 2012. I lamented this dangerous situation in my book 'The Day America Died.' It was perfectly clear to me at that time where he planned to take us.

My next input will be a specific list of actions taken in this great country, this country that once was our delight, to make Jews and Christians 'flee to the wilderness.' The signs are all in place and Barack Obama moves closer to his historical appointed destiny.

God bless America.

12

Helping Our Enemies

Hillary Clinton said the five released super-terrorists were a danger only to Afghanistan and Pakistan - not a danger to the United States. Why would someone who aspires to be president of the United States say something as absurd as that on a national television program? Does she really believe that or did she just say something that sounded good to her millions of supporters? In any case it was a totally irresponsible statement that demonstrated no regard to the safety and security of the United States. Her comments demonstrated her lack of understanding, and it demonstrated the ideas and concepts guiding the Obama administration.

Now these five terrorists will be an even greater danger to the United States. Why? Because they will have a personal score to settle against the United States, the country they consider the Great Satan. The United States kept them out of their holy war to conquer the world too long. There must be revenge and new strategies and tactics to accelerate their goals. Their minions can deal with Afghanistan and Pakistan. Their aims now are for a greater glory.

What were they probably thinking while they spent those many years in prison guarded by American soldiers? Were they wishing they could get back to their Islamic homeland so they could shoot and behead a few hundred people in the hills and cities of which they are familiar? Or have they now learned that fear is a great weapon in itself? It affects more people than do bullets. One must imagine their new strategy will be to create fear and havoc in our country - to create a defensive panic - to withdraw to protect ourselves.

Let's consider one possibility of a panic strategy. If I can think of it certainly they have already considered it. What if: a group of five terrorists blew up a bridge on a major interstate highway and then walked up the line in the traffic backup killing everyone in their automobiles? Who could defend themselves, especially if Obama has his way and citizens are not allowed to own personal weapons? They would be slaughtered - hundreds or thousands. That would be a horrible scene, but what would happen to other citizens; would their lives change to fear on the highway? This is a simple example; there are many more sophisticated ones - those five terrorists likely are already planning them. America is their target; not Afghanistan and Pakistan.

What are logical and historical options for us to fight this danger? First, ALL Americans must be allowed and encouraged to own and carry defensive weapons - AND THE TERRORISTS MUST KNOW WE ARE ARMED. Secondly, our security depends on offensive strategies, not defense. We must go where threats are and destroy those who threaten our existence. Troy and Masada demonstrate the results of defensive strategies and tactics. Rome wasn't destroyed until it became weary and lethargic and resorted to defense. An example is Hadrian 's Wall.

God bless America.

13

Coincidence or a Sign

Strange - ironic - coincidence - or a sign? I just entered information here at AD about a new book I am writing. It's titled: 'Denied 3 Times.' When I went to sign in I had to enter 4 numbers with the sign-in procedure. I had copied the introduction to paste into the book info section. I was so startled by the sign-in numbers that I couldn't remember where I was in the process. What were my sign-in numbers? They were 7666.

Those who understand scripture know what the number 7 represents. They also know what 666 represents. This is not a made-up story. I'm sure the people at AD can confirm that sign-in. It was the last one I just made. (Added as I typed this book: this was blog number **13** in my sequential process as they were listed in order in my draft. Would you believe - the description of the 666 beast is described in Chapter **13** of the Book of Revelation.)

God bless America.

14

Obama's Special Power

Recent events, especially in Syria and Iraq, disproves Obama's spoken prognosis that basically suggests, 'if we treat the Islamic Jihadists nice they will become more moderate and loving people.' All over the world and for centuries they have proven otherwise.

Did Obama think he had some special power, some prophetic gift that would make that happen? Does he still believe he has been 'chosen and sent' to suggest everybody be nice - and it will miraculously happen? Either he is totally naive - or he is in some way giving those dog-minded radical Islamist an open path to their final destination: destruction of Jerusalem and control of the entire world. They have said it; they have written it; they have demonstrated it; they continue to die for it.

Why do Muslims feel they must conquer and destroy the Jews in Jerusalem? Other than just to kill non-Muslims their eyes are focused on an object called the 'Dome of the Rock.' It's located on the rebuilt temple mount in the city. It's really a golden dome often seen in pictures and videos. Beneath that dome really is a rock, a large boulder. That boulder holds great significance for Jews, Christians, and especially Muslims. It's the rock called the 'Foundation Stone' from which Muhammad is said to have risen to Heaven. The Arabic name of that structure is, 'Qubbat As-Sakhrah.'

Why must the radical Islamists control the entire Islamic world? Understanding the concept of the Dome of the Rock, Jerusalem, and the radicalism of their beliefs - that they consider religion - they must not leave their backs vulnerable when they begin their direct attacks on the Western world - especially the United States. When they begin their attacks on the 'great Satan' they can't be bothered by attacks from within their own territories. It's a simple and long-standing military strategy. Their total focus will be on attack tactics. Obama has just returned their five top strategic planners to them to accelerate their cause - probably with new strategies.

Obama has allowed and encouraged open borders, especially from the south. Iranian terrorists have training camps in at least two countries south of our borders. What are they waiting for? Obama's administration has lost many weapons on the southern borders. Eric Holder refuses to give any information about the status of 'Fast and Furious.' Why? Where are those weapons; are they hidden in the Arizona desert waiting for young Jihadists to come across the border, by Administration invitation, and begin their terror? Was the Boston bombings by the Tsarnaev brothers just a test case of our vulnerability? Why does it appear that Obama and his administration are refusing to thwart their efforts? To be continued: First major targets.

More information about the Dome of the Rock:
http://en.wikipedia.org/wiki/Dome_of_the_Rock

God bless America.

15

Ambassador Stevens' Death His Own Fault

Can you believe it - Hillary Clinton said Ambassador Stevens was killed in Benghazi from an act of "his own choosing." She blames him for his own death. During that interview with Diane Sawyer she basically said she saw nothing, she said nothing, and she heard nothing before, during, and after that murderous Benghazi slaughter. She said she wasn't the 'expert,' therefore she had no responsibility.

Has she forgotten the importance of that '3:00 a.m. phone call' of which she so proudly boasted she could handle if she were elected president? She has never even said where she was during that Benghazi attack. Was she being attentive to Bill, hiding under the bed, watching her favorite soap opera - what was she doing? She has never said.

At least we know Barack Obama was preparing for a fund-raising trip to Las Vegas the next day and couldn't be bothered with trivial things such as Americans being slaughtered. Perhaps he also thought, "'What difference does it make' if four or five brave Americans get killed: they're probably just five infidel Christians anyway."

I watched part of that interview with Diane Sawyer. During that interview I really could understand Clinton trying to place blame somewhere else. For most unprincipled people, especially unprincipled leaders, that's the normal approach. Place the blame somewhere else, CYA, even if you are the person in charge and the one most responsible. According to her other words regarding the deaths of those four brave Americans, "What difference does it make?" What disappointed me most is that she never expressed sorrow or remorse for those four deaths. She was concerned only about herself. So sad.

It seems Obama has followed Hillary's lead in shirking responsibility. At first, he claimed credit for rescuing Bowe Bergdahl from the terrorists. After the current blowback on releasing five super terrorists, he now says it was all Chuck Hagel's decision.

Wouldn't it be great if we had leaders of our great nation who were honest, principled, just, and God-loving in whom we could comfortably place our hope and trust? I don't care which political party - I want someone I can trust, someone who accepts responsibility, someone who knows how to lead, and someone who respects our U.S. Constitution.

God bless America.

16

The Year 2025

Before I wrote my recent novel, 'Death Drones: 2025' I couldn't decide if I wanted to write another fiction or nonfiction book. As

I'm sure many will agree, it takes a lot of time and effort to write a 300 or 400 page book, whether fiction or nonfiction. I wanted to make the best use of my time and write something I would consider meaningful and relevant. Ordinarily that means a nonfiction book.

On the other hand, I've already written all I can imagine expressing my concern about the danger Barack Obama poses toward our great nation. At the moment it seems his power and influence are being weakened from all the lies, blunders, and deceptions now being discovered and discussed - even to the level of some at high levels considering impeachment. According to the Book of Revelations, it doesn't matter if he is impeached or not, if he's the one described his power will rise again to create more havoc and disaster to our great nation. He is power hungry; he is driven; he is a great deceiver. It would put me at risk to use the exact words that imply this miraculous recovery because it's written as an analogy that implies another condition. If you are interested, read Revelations, Chapter 13, especially Verse 3.

So, what is the realism in my Death Drones novel that's applicable to this Bible reference? First is the absence of cash in the new society that will be created upon his return to influence and power. I use the year 2025 as a guess of that time frame. That's also related to Chapter 13, Verse 18. In the novel, is it realism that money will not be allowed so every person on earth can be tracked by the NSA in Utah? And with total control of everyone's actions it will be easy to target anyone who's a threat to the new world order.

The Death Drones apply to Chapter 13, Verse 13 which mentions miraculous fire from the sky. In my imagination, by the year 2025 we will have drones that can fire laser beams from the sky at any target. That target might well be anyone those in charge might consider a threat to themselves or to security in general.

Did I write a novel, or did I write a nonfiction book? I haven't decided. Read the book and decide for yourself.

God bless America.

17

What Could Terrorist Do?

What has he done! Nothing that should be a surprise. For over four years I have been writing about the danger Barack Hussein Obama poses to our great nation. One of my warning books is even titled: 'King Obama: America's Greatest Danger.' This book gives many details about Obama's support to and association with the Muslim Brotherhood. Their written and blood-pledged goal is to destroy America and Western civilization. They are not kidding or throwing words in the wind. Is Obama's support to the Muslim Brotherhood by accident - or is it purposeful? Who is this man, and what are his goals?

He has just released five dangerous and very influential terrorists back onto the battlefield to kill more innocent Americans. Now, however, they will be more dangerous, cautious and insidious. They will not go directly onto the battlefield. Now they will guide those battle actions with the knowledge they have gained about America while they were incarcerated. It's most likely their next great attacks will be on American soil. It's also very likely they will begin by creating frustration and panic within our infrastructure - not directly with bullets.

Just imagine the frustration and confusion that would be created if only ten major bridges were destroyed on our interstate system. Imagine the despair and frustration if five of our power grids were destroyed - even for a few days. And our water systems — are they important? What if cell phones and other communications were disrupted and people could not be informed of activities happening around them? Would they panic? Would these activities and this panic be the prelude to martial law? Who would be in total charge of the United States if martial law were enforced? You know that answer. America's greatest danger would be its leader. What then?

Barack Obama does not yet recognize his destiny or how dangerous he is. Clearly, he believes he is doing great things for a great cause. He speaks great words of peace and prosperity - most of which are meant to deceive his many followers, and the numbers of those deceived followers will grow. Although he is a great danger to the United States and the entire world, at this time he believes he is doing mankind a great service.

God bless America.

18

Pampering to the Lows

Inequality, fair share, higher pay, more rights, more free stuff, more encouragement of anti-Bible activity; these are the things Hillary Clinton will focus on during her upcoming quest, the unending quest, to become president of the United States. These were the foundation bricks of Barack Obama's successful drive to become president. Certainly, Hillary will not stray far from that same tactic.

It's the tactic described in George Orwell's book, '1984.' To summarize this approach: the lows are used by the middle to advance themselves to the highs. The lows think they will be advanced to the middle - but that never happens. After their users, the middle, are successful, the lows are returned back to the low status until they are used again in that same cycle. The lows NEVER advance. They are only useful tools for the more ambitious. The lows are so insignificant and predictable they are not even monitored by Orwell's Big Brother.

Her target audience will be those without ambition or aspirations, poor people, the growing uneducated population, and certain other special interest groups outside the guidance of Judeo-Christian beliefs. These are the people without a firm foundation that permits them to have self-grounded beliefs and aspirations offered by the blessing of God. How can a solid structure be built without first having a steady foundation? Most of those considered the low by Orwell don't even understand those foundational concepts so they can strive toward them.

Using the Obama model she will prey upon the weak, lazy, uneducated, and those who don't understand the underlying concepts that define socialism and capitalism - and the resulting differences of each. Too many don't understand or accept the idea that under socialism a few government leaders define success and prosperity for citizens. Under capitalism, the citizens define the purpose for government and have freedom to define success for themselves.

Those with the grounded aspirations of confidence and belief realize they must work hard to be successful - and must never stray from the guiding beacon ahead. Education, a positive attitude, and hard work are the ladders to success. Success doesn't happen by accident - it's not a choice off a silver platter. Neither are security, safety, and a life of comfort as promised by Barack Obama - and soon Hillary Clinton - to get votes to fulfill their personal ambitions of power and influence. Instead, shouldn't they guide themselves with honesty so American citizens can make the right choice about who is honorable enough to lead our great nation?

Once Barack Obama reached his high level, the lows - those who put him there - were lowered back into their lower positions just as Orwell described. Poverty and food stamps have increased since he was elected president. But he still promises. His promises are to keep that higher door open for Hillary Clinton. Her goal is to reach that high place any way she can - even off the backs and dreams of the low who will be enchanted to support her. She has a great smile and great words designed to deceive those lows who pledge total allegiance to her.

Will the lows be better off if and when Hillary Clinton were to be elected president? History reveals they will be disappointed and disregarded - but they will still dream of their savior doing great things for them. Shades of George Orwell and '1984.'

The other more dire option must also be considered. Obama has demonstrated time and again that he does not respect the United States Constitution and our country's laws. Will he step aside at the end of his term to allow Hillary to campaign? Trends, and his actions, suggest he will not.

God bless America.

19

An Imperial Presidency

In many of my recent blogs, and in three of my books, I have made the idea very clear that I believe our freedoms in America will be severely restricted under the guise of protecting us from encroaching terrorism. I believe this is particularly true under the presidency of Barack Obama. Clearly, he has an insatiable thirst for personal power, as indicated by his 'phone' and his 'pen' of which he so proudly boasted.

Yesterday I was surprised to see an article by Jonathan Turley in the current American Legion magazine that said essentially the same words, only his words were better written - and with references. Turley is a law professor at George Washington University and often appears before Congress. This is part of his article, titled, 'The United States is at grave risk of embracing an imperial presidency':

"When James Madison shaped a new constitutional system for the United States, he and his fellow framers had one overriding fear: tyranny.

They wanted to divide power between three branches and create lines of separation that prevented the concentration of power in any single branch. The framers based their ideas on an understanding of human nature - and human weakness. They tried to create a system in which ambition would check ambition. However, they knew that citizens can be distracted or deceived into giving up their very freedom. Madison warned future generations that 'if Tyranny and Oppression come to this land, it will be in the guise of fighting a foreign enemy.' The framers knew how effective fear can be to induce citizens to give up their liberties. Recent years have proven them once again prophetic in their warnings.

---- Despite these warnings, many people have embraced largely unchecked presidential powers under the assurance that the rising security state will keep them safe."

My blog on 5-28 discussed this issue and asked the same question. How far will we give up our freedom in the name of protecting ourselves? How far will the government go to use that threat of fear against us to increase their personal power?

God bless America.

20

Patriot or Traitor

Edward Snowden: patriot or traitor? I heard this question asked this morning in a clip from a program scheduled to be aired tonight on NBC News.

Many of us have asked this same question. Our opinions about this man are certainly varied and are guided by our backgrounds, our experiences, our prejudices and our political leanings. So far, I can't get a firm fix on my opinion of this man. My vacillation, however, is not based on Snowden's actions or intentions. My opinion is based on my trust or distrust about the intentions of our government, specifically Barack Obama.

My big dilemma of trust or distrust is: which one of these men poses the greatest danger to America? Edward Snowden is just one man who can be classified as a traitor. Do his actions so far suggest he's a man determined to harm America, or simply trying to alert citizens to the serious dangers posed by our government? On the other hand, Barack Obama has the power and platform to preserve a great nation - or destroy it. How can a man who tells so many lies and falsehoods be trusted to fulfill his sworn duty? Do actions and comments always reveal intentions?

Could one imagine Snowden plans great harm to America? Could one imagine Barack Obama plans great harm to our freedoms and democracy? What are some clues?

So far, as far as we know, Snowden has released only information that alerts us to the depths of government spying against American citizens, especially that data gathered at the new NSA spy center in Bluffdale, Utah. If left unchecked, how far would the government go to delve into every corner of every citizens' lives - in the name of fighting terrorism? Unchecked, likely there would be no stopping them until all our freedoms have been suppressed.

And, what do we know about the Obama administration? Lies, deceptions, falsehoods, cover-ups, denials, and more restrictions every day that limit our freedoms. They are Obama's 'pen' and new daily regulations that bypass our leaders in Congress, duly elected to protect our freedom. Why are they bypassing that check and balance system designed to protect us?

So, who presents the most danger to our great nation? Is Edward Snowden the traitor?

My latest book: 'Death Drones 2025,' gives a description of the danger of allowing a government to delve too deeply into every person's private lives - especially their everyday purchases, which the NSA will have the capability to do when we convert to a cashless society. Coming soon?

God bless America.

21

Cultural Resistence

I'm still reformatting many of my books into Smashwords. While working on an old book, 'The Peer Pressure Monster,' I ran across this statement about personal responsibility and personal aspirations. I decided to share it here on this blog. The new title on Smashwords will be, 'The Dream Slayer.' Smashwords explained how to include the graphics I didn't have on the other digital sites. Maybe I can use the same formatting for those sites and resubmit those to include the graphics. I'm almost finished this formatting for Smashwords and will have it posted there within the next two days. Below is the extraction I rediscovered:

"Cultural Resistance: Although most people probably prefer to be successful, many prefer the comfort and security of what they know and understand. An existence, even a low-level existence, is known and understood. Improvement and advancement are unknown, therefore they become vague risks. Although common sense and simple logic should be enough to encourage someone to try to become successful, the comfort and security of what's already known and understood has a strong appeal.

Additionally, members of lower cultures strongly depend on each other for survival; food, shelter, transportation, and small loans. If someone doesn't have a job that person always has a family member or a close friend who will provide and share those basic necessities.

This situation explains one of the workplace mysteries concerning the work ethic and reliability of lower cultured workers. It would be logical to believe members of lower cultures would be reliable and hard workers to protect their jobs. However, that's not the usual case. Many of these workers show little concern for work for they know there's always another way to survive that requires less work. This low work ethic, reinforced by cultural interdependency, is another of those weaknesses that makes a person vulnerable to normal peer pressure.

Cultural resistance has another face. To escape from a lower culture to become successful one must intentionally and purposefully rise above his or her current aspiration level. This purposeful effort demands a rejection of behavioral and social values that only the strongest members of that cultural group are able to achieve. One must abandon many of his or her values and beliefs which often results in the loss of friends and close associates.

The statement, "Birds of a feather flock together," applies to this process, for when one attempts to become more successful that person also attempts to rise to a higher social class. This abdication and rejection of those values and beliefs of one's culture create rifts and conflicts that pressure a person to remain in his or her normal place. This pressure not to become *better* than the reference group forces many to reject plans and aspirations for personal success.

These internal barriers to their own aspirations must be removed before society squanders money, effort, and time on job training, educational opportunities, and physical amenities to improve the financial and social opportunities for these lower-cultured and disadvantaged citizens. It will continue to be useless and futile to offer opportunities and advantages to members of these groups until they free themselves from these cultural pressures, and learn to form their own personal ideologies and value judgments.

The first step to resolve this social problem, which is a major economic problem for society, is to create openness and honesty before offering training or assistance. Those targeted for training or assistance must understand and acknowledge that their personal success is determined more by their ability to reject their culture and values than by any external support they receive. That external support will remain useless, futile, and wasted until those targeted members learn to overcome those self-imposed internal constraints."

God bless America.

22

A Book Along the Way

Two weeks ago I returned from another driving trip, from Mississippi to California, to visit our children and grandchildren. I retired from the Air Force there in 1978, so that's still their home. Their numbers have blossomed from: children, grandchildren, and now 3 great-grandchildren. Years ago my job moved me back to Mississippi, where my wife and I remained. We are originally from this area and still have relatives nearby. Since we are now the eldest in our two families, we decided to remain here in case the others needed help.

During the driving trip to California and back two things reminded me of my writings and the events happening in our great nation. In my book: 'America 20XX,' I fictionally wrote that Islamic terrorists were infiltrating into the U.S. through the desert south of Casa Grande, Arizona, to become pre-positioned moles waiting for a certain event to occur before they became active infiltrators. Two weeks after I published that book, Border Patrol agents found an Islamic book titled, 'In Memory of our Martyrs' in that same desert in that same location I had described. During that trip I stayed one night at a hotel in Casa Grande and had time to look south and wonder if that idea could really become real. Why was that book found in that location?

I also had another surprise, something new, which reminded me of my latest novel, 'Death Drones 2025.' Each of the eight times I registered at a hotel I was asked for my driver's license. At first I thought it was only to match the name with the name on my credit card to insure it wasn't a stolen credit card. I was surprised when the clerk entered my license number into the computer. This wasn't random - it was all eight times. I wondered once my identity was confirmed - why did they need to enter my license number? Then it struck me up side the head like a bazooka: the NSA and Bluffdale, Utah. I have no doubt this information went straight into the limitless information storage center there. My first inclination was to say, "Who cares?" But then reality and ideas from my book slapped me right in the face. Everything the government does is important - and it leads to further encroachment on our freedoms. I asked, "Could the next step be that described in my book for total government control of every citizen?"

That next step before total government control (totalitarianism) is a cashless society. Since everything and everybody will be controlled by numbers and computers - why is cash necessary?

Keep watching. When the government says we no longer need cash it will sound like a wonderful and rational idea, and will be readily accepted by many. And it might be. But the bigger question becomes: what happens next? This link takes you to the NSA Bluffdale Center.

http://en.wikipedia.org/wiki/Utah_Data_Center

God bless America.

23

A Wasted Society

I'm editing an old book for a new submission to Smashwords, and just crossed this section of that book: 'The Peer Pressure Monster.' I found it even more interesting than when I wrote it several years ago. This is that section:

Peer pressure against personal work performance was one of my greatest surprises when I entered the work environment after graduating from high school. I clearly remember that for every word or act of motivation and encouragement from my superiors, I got twice as many admonitions from my peers that I should not be different from them. Many peers were much older than myself which gave them influence and credibility. A person who hasn't experienced this pressure doesn't understand the despair and apprehension placed upon a person who begins work life with aspirations of becoming successful. Adult peer pressure takes a more subtle form that doesn't openly show itself, but instead works by the force of innuendo and suggestion, often without words ever being spoken.

Peer pressure is not just a personal problem; it also creates productivity problems and socio-economic problems. On a personal level it forces susceptible people to be less than they can be. It robs them of their aspirations as well as their maximum contributions to society. Negative peer pressure in the work environment is similar to theft in that environment. A person is hired to contribute his or her best performance on a job. Anyone who's forced to contribute less than he or she ordinarily would contribute gives less than the work contract requires. For example, if a worker would ordinarily work at eighty percent of his or her maximum capability, and peer pressure forces that person to contribute only seventy percent, that workplace has been robbed of ten percent of expected productivity. Would a company allow workers to steal ten percent of the physical assets or money and just watch it happen? Management experts generally agree worker productivity is only fifty percent of most workers' real capabilities.

Peer pressure also creates socio-economic problems. Excluding the negative impact peer pressure has on our youth, which itself is a major concern, peer pressure creates loss of jobs and condemns many disenfranchised citizens to remain in poverty and despair. Economic opportunity is developed through the creation of jobs. Other than through inheritance or random luck at the blackjack table or slot machine, there is no other legal way to gain economic progress. From a practical and realistic view, jobs are the only sources to economic success and survival for most people.

Negative peer pressure in the workplace places those jobs in jeopardy. Any productivity weakness by any person in a workplace causes that product or service to be more expensive. For example, if a worker paid $8.00 an hour produces two items an hour, each item has a direct labor cost of $4.00. If that worker is forced by peer pressure to make only one item an hour, the direct labor cost for each item becomes $8.00. If the standard labor cost for that item is $6.00, that workplace will not be profitable. If unprofitable, it can't remain in business as a viable social or economic function.

If a workplace isn't profitable and competitive it will cease to exist and those jobs will be lost. Lost jobs result in lost opportunities for individuals, and a greater burden on all other members of society to support those people who lose those jobs. The socio-economic problem is often compounded, for many people who lose jobs also lose hope and aspirations, and become content to be supported through welfare and other human support systems. What a tragedy for themselves and what a waste for society.

God bless America.

24

Considering Equality

I've spent a lot of time lately, at least the past two or three years, writing serious blogs. My main focus has been on politics and how I perceive Barack Obama as being one not serving in the best interests of our great nation. And, it's obvious he spews many great deceptive words that many people worship. A certain Book suggests a man will arrive speaking these many words aimed to deceive.

His most profound words are to propose we should have a great redistribution of wealth without the presence of God to provide those great blessings. Just yesterday I read an article that stated another man of great respect world-wide proposes that same concept for world economic equalization. This man occupies a great position that acknowledges God. Could this mean - now there is a first supported by the second?

To escape some of these serious questions, perhaps even biblical questions, I decided to revisit my fairy tale book characters for a less serious setting. In my book, 'Wishing Wells and Broken Tales,' there were many characters I left to their own destinies. For example, when I finished that book, Slowee the turtle who thought he was a rabbit, and Hippity the rabbit who liked to race, were still together. They raced often and Hippity always won except when he didn't want Slowee to feel bad. To make them equal in the book, perhaps I should have put a heavy shell on Hippity's back so he couldn't be faster than Slowee. That way they could be equal so neither could win a race. Or would that be fair to Hippity? Would that even be fair to Slowee?

On the other hand, if Hippity had a heavy shell so he would be as slow as Slowee, how could he dash about finding good grazing places where he and Slowee could both have the best food and nourishment? Perhaps if I went back and made that change in their story both might perish because Hippity couldn't exercise all his talents. Or perhaps I should just leave them alone so they can each find their own paths to success and happiness. After all, Slowee is a turtle, and Hippity is a rabbit. Would Slowee just get fat and lazy, and lose his feeling of a purpose in life if he were robbed of his turtle aspirations?

I wish I knew the answers to these questions. Perhaps the actions of number one and number two, identified above, will eventually make any decisions on my part unnecessary.

God bless America.

25

Dropouts and Incarceration

We are a country of laws, but are we a country of reason and common sense? We spend billions of dollars to incarcerate non-violent offenders, especially drug related, while we have no programs to keep many of those offenders from resorting to desperate acts that lead to their incarceration. Our leaders focus on controlling the uncontrollable output, not on preparing the input for a productive life. That input must be controlled through education results. The concept of 'dropout' must be eliminated.

This is some information from the U.S. Department of Education, National Center for Education Statistics. (2013). The Condition of Education 2013 (NCES 2013-037), Status Dropout Rates:

"The status dropout rate declined from 12 percent in 1990 to 7 percent in 2011. Reflecting the overall decline in the status dropout rate between 1990 and 2011, the rates also declined for Whites (from 9 percent to 5 percent), Blacks (from 13 percent to 7 percent), and Hispanics (from 32 percent to 14 percent). Over this period, the status dropout rate was lowest for Whites, followed by Blacks and Hispanics. For example, in 2011, the status dropout rate for Whites (5 percent) was lower than the status dropout rates for Blacks (7 percent) and Hispanics (14 percent). The gap between Whites and Hispanics narrowed from 23 percentage points in 1990 to 9 percentage points in 2011; the gaps between Whites and Blacks in these two years were not measurably different.

The "status dropout rate" represents the percentage of 16- through 24-year-olds who are not enrolled in school and have not earned a high school credential (either a diploma or an equivalency credential such as a General Educational Development [GED] certificate). Data are based on sample surveys of the civilian non-institutionalized population, which excludes persons in prisons, persons in the military, and other persons not living in households. Data for all races include other racial/ethnic categories not separately shown. Race categories exclude persons of Hispanic ethnicity."

Note: this information from the Department of Education is from select sample surveys. Analyzing data by state and locality, which I have done many times as data for my education research, the statistics are greatly different. The real average drop-out rate nationwide is closer to 25 percent. Certain urban communities have drop-out rates as high as 80 percent. Other research states that over 95 percent of those incarcerated are school dropouts.

From Wikipedia: the incarceration rate in the United States of America is the highest in the world. As of 2009, the incarceration rate was 743 per 100,000 of national population (0.743%).[2] While the United States represents about 5 percent of the world's population, it houses around 25 percent of the world's prisoners. Imprisonment of America's 2.3 million prisoners, costing $24,000 per inmate per year, and $5.1 billion in new prison construction, consumes $60.3 billion in budget expenditures. According to a 2014 report by Human Rights Watch, "tough-on-crime" laws adopted since the 1980s have filled U.S. prisons with mostly nonviolent offenders.

The answer to our social, economic, and crime problems is very simple. We must not let students leave school without being prepared to participate in a normal society. This means, first and foremost, they must be able to read. It's been my observation long ago as a student, and more recently as a teacher, that those most vulnerable to drop-out are those students who can't read well.

Those test scores and statistics that make educators look good must be ignored. We must not allow a student to leave school without being prepared to participate positively in our society. We must teach them how to read. If they can read they can become part of our productive society.

God bless America, and our students.

26

Who Are Racists

Just wondering. Recently, there have been many bloggers, 'letter to the editor' writers and 'sound off' writers strongly proposing that Republicans are racists because most refused to vote for and support Obama. Just wondering: If Democrats supported their Democratic candidate and refused to vote for a black Republican candidate - would that prove Democrats are also racists? Probably not. It would probably prove only that the candidate had chosen his or her voters before making a decision of which party to belong. Racism probably is not determined by political party or the color of one's skin. There are black racists as well as white, yellow, and blue racists. Why do those Obama worshipers continue this radical claim?

It's because Obama and his ardent supporters have been well trained in the 12 rules for radicals outlined by Saul Alinsky. Obama was trained in this doctrine while he was a member of the Gamaliel Foundation, and taught it while he was a 'community organizer.' One of those rules is to keep the opponent off guard with outrageous charges. Perhaps to counter this Alinsky claim of racism, Republicans could equally mount a stronger offensive claiming that Democrats want to keep everyone poor so they can be more easily controlled.

Just wondering: could this be a valid claim, or could it be one of those Alinsky 12 rules for radicals? Anyway, does name-calling ever serve a worthwhile purpose? Perhaps the aims and actions of a person are stronger indicators of a person's intentions and character than what one occasionally says or miss-speaks. Words can be twisted by anyone.

God bless America - including Democrats, Republicans, and Independents.

27

I Love Casa Grande, Arizona

I just returned from another driving trip to California from my home here in Mississippi - 2350 miles. My last military assignment was at the Defense Depot in Tracy, California. That's also where my son and daughter finished school, and consider home. Consequently; kids, grand-kids, and great-grand-kids are all still in the Stockton-Modesto area. Along the way we consider it only four or five one-day trips instead of one long trip. It seems less formidable that way.

Anyway, when we turned onto I-8 from I-10 at Casa Grande, AZ - to take the Phoenix bypass from Gila Bend to Buckeye, on Highway 85, I immediately thought of my book: 'America 20XX: The New World Order.' The story begins in the desert south of that area. This is the area where the Iranian book titled: 'In Memory of our Martyrs' was found by Homeland Security agents on January 28, 2011. I had just published my book at Amazon on January 2. My book detailed how Islamic terrorists were entering the U.S. at that very same spot to preposition for an attack when the right time arrives. I don't think that time has arrived yet.

The book also suggests how easy it would be for terrorists to transfer and conceal weapons until their designated time arrives. Several examples are given in the book.

We also drove past El Paso along the way. Another scene in the book details how weapons might easily be moved into the U.S. at El Paso to preposition for planned terrorist use. We always stop in El Paso to spend the night. Looking across the river at all those lights is like looking at stars in an endless sky.

We had a great trip to California, and enjoyed all the scenery along the way. But along the way, I always wonder what dangers keep crossing our southern borders, especially between El Paso and Casa Grande. I'll probably make the same trip next year - but hopefully later in the year when we can travel I-40. The scenery and colors are much more beautiful on I-40.

These two links give more information about the Islamic book and the drug-weapons tunnels.

http://factsnotfairies.blogspot.com/2011/01/in-memory-of-our-martyrs-in-az-desert.html

http://www.huffingtonpost.com/2013/10/31/mexico-drug-tunnel_n_4183476.html

God bless America.

28

An Uneducated Society

The goals of our current government require an *uneducated* society. Therefore, government must not be trusted to educate our children. Nearly a third of American students drop out of school because student success now occupies no concern in American education. An educated society threatens a government not guided by Constitutional principles. To protect America, parents must hold fast to the important responsibility of educating their children.

It's self-evident that our education system is failing American students. This failure has at least four sources.

First, the defined purpose for education has been skewed and blurred during the past two generations. Originally, education was recognized as preparation for literacy and jobs. To accomplish this goal, education was focused on reading, writing and comprehension; with a leaning toward job preparation. Currently, education is designed only to make the designers of education programs appear successful. Education is not designed for a student's purpose or a specific goal. Without a clear goal, how can the goal ever be reached?

Second, traditional family composition has been devastated during the past several years, especially since the inception of the 'Great Society.' Now, as many children are born to be raised by one parent as by two parents. A void has been created in America's social structure that has created a void in the education structure. When a child has been abandoned by one of two parents how can that child ever feel fully supported - and important enough to strive for excellence? A government does not raise children; that's a family duty and responsibility, and creation's norm.

Third, the current government administration under Barack Hussein Obama is more focused on social justice, economic equality, and government control than on individual and personal success. Success of the many, society, cannot be achieved without first there being successful individuals. Success and education are individual things. There must be those who see themselves as more successful so others may see that opportunity - that door to freedom and happiness. The vision espoused by Obama is for everyone to be equal, thereby meaning mediocre - or less. Barack Obama has never focused any comments on individual and personal success for individuals. Waiting for a free handout, and having more children for a larger free handout, are not great education enhancement plans.

Fourth, our current education system is designed for failure - that's failure in regard to what most successful people interpret as the purpose for education. That self-understanding is to prepare for a job, thereby resulting in prosperity, comfort, and happiness. Our current education plans are designed to support and facilitate the coming new world order. Under that NWO we are to all be equal -

so social and economic justice will prevail on the entire earth.

Education is a personal thing and a family responsibility. To help with that task I've written a book offered FREE to anyone who wants it. *'Positive Learning Skills'* is a revised book that gives parental skills and student study skills to help fulfill that responsibility. We must not allow the government to determine our individual and personal success. It's too personal and valuable.

This FREE book is available now only at Smashwords - and it's free as a digital download. It can also be read free online and copied to your computer, so you don't need a special reader. This is the link:

https://www.smashwords.com/books/view/432794

29

The Great Tribulation

Have you noticed the current war on Christians? Christianity, Christians, and those who believe in Jesus and God are being persecuted and killed all over the world. Even here in America there is a direct war on Christians and any references to God or the Christian religion. This war is no longer subtle - it's now direct and forceful. Even the president of this great nation, the one who should lead under the same principles and belief of God that guided the foundation of America said, "We are no longer a Christian nation."

When I was young, 50 to 60 years ago - I was born in 1939; no one would have openly rejected or criticized God or the Christian religion. It was America's foundation. There was a great openness of God's guidance and protection. It was a continuation of the foundation of America; everyone knew the formation, strength and power of our America was allowed through the guidance of His power. Otherwise, how could America have become the guiding beacon for world peace? Over the last few years that has changed - and that change is accelerating. There is a Bible prophesy for this change. The prophet John described this change in his vision described in the Bible book of Revelation.

This review by Propheysysigns.com is taken from Revelation 12: 17. It's #16 of 20 prophesy signs.

Reference: "Then the dragon was enraged at the woman and went off to make war against the rest of her offspring--those who obey God's commandments and hold to the testimony of Jesus Christ.

What it looks like:

Throughout history, Satan, the Dragon, has abused mankind, and specifically the Woman, the nation Israel, in an attempt to kill the Messiah. During the End Times, this persecution will intensify, and Satan will become laser-focused in his final persecution of the Woman and her final offspring, the Church. These verses clearly teach the Church will endure the Great Tribulation. Why does God allow this attack upon His Bride? As He has throughout the history of the Church, God allows persecution and suffering in our lives in order to purify believers and make the Church stronger.

The Church and Israel will have a difficult time during the reign of terror of the Antichrist and the False Prophet. All out spiritual war commences when Satan will be cast out of heaven to this earth. We will be called to remain patient during this 3 ½ year period, which is a relatively short time. We are called to be faithful, keep his commandments and some will have the high privilege of being martyrs as they hold to their testimony of Jesus during the Great Tribulation." End of reference.

Perhaps the end times are not here, but this accelerating attack on Christianity and the Church certainly suggests the Woman, the Church and Christianity, will soon be fleeing to the wilderness to survive. Revelation, Chapter 12.

God bless America.

30

Would Our Government Fire on Innocent Civilians?

In two of my blogs in 2013, I asked the question - would our military fire on civilians if they were ordered to do so by Obama's government? This is a very, very serious question. My conclusion was - yes they would. They would have no choice, because those civilians would be classified as 'terrorists' by Obama's government.

One of those blogs reported an email I got from a friend that discussed the same question. Supposedly the contents forwarded were written by a retired military general. In it he discusses this question with an active duty Army colonel. This is that forwarded email:

"Keep your uniform clean---I think we're going to need you! When I asked my colleague the Army Colonel why he thinks Obama is doing this, the reply I received from this life-long soldier and Army leader shocked me. Paraphrasing him, this is what he told me in a nut shell. He said, most branches of the service routinely engage in war games and come up with strategies and tactics on how to handle every type of military conflict and scenario that can be imagined. One of the big new battle scenarios being actively discussed in the military recently is how to handle civil unrest in the U.S. And fighting in the streets. What will the Army do if called in to fight armed civilians in the streets of the United States? How will that urban warfare be conducted? Will troops be able to fire upon other American citizens when the troops take an oath to protect American citizens?

He said many in the military are discussing the very real possibility that Obama will attempt to stay in office beyond two terms. It is being speculated that Obama will do this by declaring a state of martial law. The easiest way to declare martial law is when there is massive civil unrest and riots throughout the U.S. Thus, it is believed that Obama, and his regime, will intentionally create a situation of massive civil unrest. Some believe he has already started to implement that strategy by forcing Obamacare on everyone (when the populace did not ask for it and less than 300 people in power voted for it). End of quote.

I also reported several times that Obama's administration would justify firing on American citizens by proclaiming certain groups as 'terrorists.' Did you hear what Senator Reed called the people in Nevada? He called them 'domestic terrorists.' Weapons were pointed and ready to fire. Only massive media coverage stopped the possible carnage. Perhaps that media coverage will not be enough to stop it next time after Obama and Reed convince the American people that those Americans standing up for American beliefs really are terrorists. How many loyal Americans will agree with the Obama administration that they should be fired upon - killed - wiped out? Why are there now many armed agents in non-military branches of our federal government? Didn't Obama once say, "We need a civilian security force as powerful as our military?" What is the purpose of his armed security force?

God bless America.

31
Silent Killing by Drones

Regarding the grazing standoff in Nevada, a recent news article states, "Tensions simmered Tuesday in the standoff between federal land managers and a Nevada rancher -- but the feds are being coy about how far they'll go to pursue Cliven Bundy as both sides regroup for their next move."

Recently large groups of armed ranchers and supporters of Cliven Bundy's right to graze his cattle on federal land faced a large group of armed federal agents on the grazing site were he lets his cattle graze. Fortunately, no shots were fired from either side to initiate a great tragedy such as those of Ruby Ridge or the Branch Davidians in Waco. In those two events American citizens were killed by federal agents. In both cases, none of those killed were ever officially charged with any illegal activity. These two events were examples that suggest the federal government will use deadly force by accident - if not by design - to prove the power of the federal government.

Now, the federal government has to face American citizens face-to-face when they commit deadly force. In this event, those activities are open to media publicity. But, what if? What if deadly force could be used without that face-to-face confrontation? What if that deadly force by the government were committed by drones - very quiet drones?

My latest book, 'Death Drones 2025' details events when these drones will be used against innocent American citizens. When I wrote the book, I imagined this possibility happening in the year 2025. This is only year 2014. Has the federal government already developed this capability? Will they use it against citizens they target for more subtlety and secrecy? They have already proved they will fire on innocent citizens. Why should they hesitate now, especially if they have special weapons to avoid the media's exposure of the face-to-face carnage? Those weapons are coming - if they are not already here.

God bless America.

32

Obama's Henchmen

Susan Rice and Samantha Power are currently in the national news for their opinions and statements. It seems they continue their activities and words that discredit our great nation. Hopefully, they and their great leader will fail in their aim to destroy our national credibility. Their ideologies and opinions have been well known for a long time. Below is an excerpt from my book, 'The Day America Died,' concerning these two. My book also discloses the backgrounds of many others Obama keeps close. This excerpt was before they were appointed to their current positions.

"Susan Rice, the United States ambassador to the United Nations, also has a long record of ideas opposing the interests of the United States. She firmly believes that the United States should follow the dictates and aims of the United Nations although much of that idealism is extremely anti-United States, and favors those extremists who would do great harm to our country. Even as a member of UNICEF she has taken actions that have aided known terrorists. While ambassador to Sudan under the Clinton Administration, she allegedly did not acknowledge Sudan's offer to hand over Osama Bin Laden who had already initiated terrorist acts against the United States even before the 9/11 attack in New York. Had she cooperated with the Sudanese at that time, would that have prevented that tragic attack on the United States and the loss of over 3000 innocent lives?

At that time she didn't think Al-Qaeda was a threat, and blamed George Bush for creating problems by not giving his full cooperation to the United Nations, although the U.N. doesn't stop wars and it doesn't sanction terrorist organizations. Still supporting her 'the terrorists didn't do it' ideas, she recently announced to the world that terrorists did not initiate the attack on the consulate annex in Benghazi. Before those words barely dripped from her mouth, it was proven that the attack was initiated and carried out by recognized terrorists. Her defense for her initial response was that was the best information available at the time.

This invites the question: why was there a big rush to announce the big lie? Why not wait until more information was gathered before making such a strong statement against what really happened in Benghazi? Would a few more hours to get the truth have hurt the cause of the Obama campaign? That was her and the administration's only concern. Win the election; not let the truth prevail.

Samantha Power of the National Security Council might be considered the most extreme of Obama's appointees and advisors. She is extremely anti-Israel and suggests that Israel is the source of most problems in the Middle East. In an interview in 2002 she even said Israel should be invaded to force them to allow Palestine to set up a separate state. She also does not believe Iran is preparing a nuclear weapon and does not pose a real threat to its neighbors.

According to other reports she was also involved with the recent Libya event that resulted in the death of four Americans by Islamic terrorists. Her husband is the recently departed Regulatory Czar, Cass Sunstein. Clearly, Samantha Power is a real danger to the security of the United States by any exercise of power or influence in or near the White House."

With supporters like these - who needs enemies?

God bless America.

33

Reply to Attacker

Thank you for your review of 'The Day America Died.' Yes, I am an old white male (75 years old - and very proud of it thank you.) I've never been accused of being racist before, but I guess that's your choice of name-calling if that's what you prefer. Ordinarily, that's a label one uses when there's no other real and valid - and provable observation. It's the label of last resort. I never place a label on any person - even my worst enemy, if I had any enemies. (This is the Alinsky tactic of always keeping the opposition on the defensive. You will never trick me into this one.)

Your attack on me is straight out of the Saul Alinsky book, which most of Obama's 'Pied Piper' unquestioning followers seem to follow - without question. I have serious questions about this man because I believe he means great danger to our nation. I'm especially concerned since I served 21 years in the U.S. military to defend the principles of this great nation. Although your comments seem to convey the idea that America should be equal to all other nations of the world, I don't believe that for an instant. The idealism of America has always been greatness, or leading us in that direction of greatness.

American progress has always been led by the idea of God-given greatness. Without that idealism guiding America why should young students care about their individual success and strive to improve themselves with education? Without that idealism, why should parents care about the success of their children; why should citizens care about the success and happiness of our friends and neighbors; why should we care about anything other than being robots following along with the idealism that we should all just be average and equal? As you so succinctly expressed in your review - that's where Obama wants to take us - and you totally agree with his goal.

Don't you have any feeling or inclination that God put you here on this earth to do something, not just to sit back and be average and equal? Why on earth would you place your trust and confidence in a man who routinely speaks falsehoods and lies to lead the gullible along that 'Pied Pipers' path?

You are absolutely correct in your observation that I do not trust Barack Hussein Obama and his plans for America and the world. If his plans were honorable - his words would be truthful. If you think this book is really tilted against Obama, then you should read, 'King Obama: America's Greatest Danger.' This one is my best seller. I'm sure you will just love it.

Again, thank you for your review. I wish you well, success, happiness, and more than just equality in everything you do.

Will Clark
(An old man - and a proud American still trying to serve the principles upon which America was founded.)

God bless America.

34

The New Reality?

Below is part of a review that was just posted regarding my book, 'The Day America Died.' I think this belief expressed in this review about our great nation, is being accepted by more people. It's also expresses an outlook that America is no longer a great nation, therefore young people should not strive for greater success. This analysis implies we Americans should be satisfied just being equal with others in the world. I don't think that's what our Founders intended. It's certainly not my outlook toward our great nation. Perhaps this was the outlook espoused by Vladimir Lenin and the Bolsheviks when they equalized Russia. We are not Bolsheviks, we are Americans. Excerpt below:

"The world is now a better place in spite of the wars and many insurrections of people moving ever closer to democratic governments based largely on the American ideal you hold so dear. The equalization of the world's economies, especially India and China, will make the United States just one of the players in the world we live in, no longer the superior giant that won World War II, but a place of peace and relative prosperity.

As for all those people getting handouts. The outsourcing of jobs (equalizing income worldwide), and increasing automation with computers and robots eliminating jobs continually, means that the easy route to a "job" is no longer available. There is plenty of work to do, but most of it will not pay well. In order for the United

States economy to improve, people must have income. One way people can have income is to be paid for creative activity and social good deeds. The skewing of incomes between the lowest wage earners and the highest does a disservice to fairness and the American ideal of "equality." But it is happening at an ever-increasing rate. The rich are getting richer and at this point the majority of Americans are slipping into poverty. You seem to equate poverty with poor education and laziness. That's an old saw about young people that never has been true. Over half of the working, taxpaying citizens of the United States are slipping rapidly into poverty while working. If they lose their job, they can't get another one except one that pays much less.

Stop blaming the President and understand the real problems we are facing. If you do not, I can only conclude that you are one of those old male white racist Americans who can't understand why the tremendous power that you held over inferiors like immigrants, those not of the white race, and women in the 20th century is slipping away in the 21st. It's time you get over it and understand the new reality." End.

I have two concluding comments regarding this review:

1. Barack Obama has done absolutely nothing to help create jobs or inspire young people. His policies have eliminated many good jobs - especially through his energy policies. He speaks only of equality - as in the days of Lenin.

2. I have analyzed the education-poverty relationship for over twenty years. Without fail - without a single blip - pockets of failing education and poverty always - always - go together. An area of low average education attainment always - always has a matching poverty level. This can be analyzed in any 'World Almanac and Book of Facts,' which I have done for the past

twenty years. These data are also included in my book, 'The Education Jungle.'

I do thank the distinguished professor for his review. But, what other outlook should one expect from a college professor?

God bless America.

35
Keeping Them Controlled

This is an excerpt from George Orwell's book, '1984.' In the book, Orwell explains there are three tiers of citizens in Oceania, one of the three major divisions of the world. There were those who controlled the government 'Big Brother,' those who wanted to rise to their place, and the Low. The Low were called Proles. This was Orwell's reference to the proletariat, referring to the 'rise of the proletariat' at that time in Russia. The proletariat was also identified as 'the working class.'

Orwell explained further that the High, and those who wanted to take their place, always used the Proles to achieve their goals. Once their goals were achieved, the Proles never received what they expected from the purge, and were always cast back down to the position of the Low. They never rose above that regardless who was in power. This extract defines Orwell's Proles:

"So long as they (the Proles) continued to work and breed, their other activities were without importance. Left to themselves, like cattle turned loose upon the plains of Argentina, they had reverted to a style of life that appeared to be natural to them, a sort of ancestral pattern...Heavy physical work, the care of home and children, petty quarrels with neighbors, films, football, beer and above all, gambling filled up the horizon of their minds. To keep them in control was not difficult."

Clearly, Obama took a cue from this definition of Proles. Instead of Proles, Obama has his great following of Doles, whom he finds not difficult to keep them in control. All he has to do, as he has always done, is promise them more free stuff. His first campaign began with the slogan, 'fair share.' This meant they would get more free stuff. Then he went further and said we would 'share the wealth.' This was also Vladimir Lenin's promise to his Proletariat - and they supported him to destroy Russia. Obama knows that all he has to do is promise free handouts, those doles, to his followers and TO KEEP THEM IN CONTROL IS NOT DIFFICULT.

Obama keeps promising them, his Doles, free stuff and a fair share. He has never once, never, never, made a speech where he encouraged his Doles to stay in school, get an education, get a job, pay taxes, and become a real American citizen, accepting all those expectations and responsibilities as an American citizen.

But, he will never do that. Apparently it's not too difficult to keep them in control with all his promises of what he will give them. He has had five years to improve their lives - their lives have gotten even WORSE - as George Orwell described. There are more people on food stamps than ever before, and more jobs have been eliminated for young black men.

Obama's new mantra is 'Income Equality.' That's clearly another promise to keep his Proles (Doles) in line. This is another promise that will never be fulfilled - until the Doles decide to do more to advance themselves. That will never happen under Obama. He will keep promising - and they will keep doing his bidding. His followers will blindly follow anywhere he leads them. Let's hope one day it might be in a positive direction.

God bless America.

36

Education Must Not Be Ignored

Another observation introduced by that study(The EEOS Coleman Report) is the idea that, from an economic and productivity viewpoint, we might get more direct results from our taxes if some of the money we spend on education were spent on job experience and on-the-job training. This question is particularly applicable, today, since current major policies regarding education tend to suggest the purpose for education is to increase direct job skills for new workers entering the workforce.

Certainly, education should give a student more than employer desirability. But, if education policies are made on the premise that education is to develop and promote job skills, then why not spend our tax dollars on functions that will directly develop those skills?

Simply, if we need more computer technicians, why not train those students who want to become computer technicians to become computer technicians? Why must they attend four years of general high school? What purpose does that serve? If the work environment needs more nurses, why not train students who want to be nurses to become nurses, instead of making them survive four years of unrelated courses in a regular high school?

In summary, the survey asked a simple and fundamental question, regarding costs of education. That is: if the purpose of education is to train students for jobs, why not use that education money to train them for jobs instead of using that money for a general education not related to jobs? This observation is not to suggest that courses that entertain and enlighten are not important to one's quality of life. However, the need to test and grade on those broadening courses should certainly be questioned. Assigning grades to courses that should be quality-of-life enhancing serves no purpose for education, and is more likely to create negativity and despair. And, it's not necessary.

That survey, in 1966, discovered that more money and resources have little influence on resulting grades and scores. The finding, generally, was that grades and scores, including SAT scores, were determined more by family and social conditions than by the amount of money spent per student.

An editorial dated September 13, 1993, by George F. Will, a columnist for The Washington Post Writers Group, said money-education results relationship has not changed. In his column, Will cited three sources documenting that spending more money for education does nothing to increase grade and test results.

He cited examples to show family composition and cost-results relationships. He referenced a 1992 book, *America's Smallest School: The Family,* by Paul Barton. It reported the proportion of single parent families has increased over the past several decades, and school performance, measured by standardized tests, has declined. As an example he cited that North Dakota had the nation's second highest proportion of students in two-parent families, and the highest scores in math. On the other hand, Washington D.C. had the highest proportion of one parent families and next to last in test scores.

Empower America and the American Exchange Legislative Council reported their findings regarding costs and related test results. They reported that from 1973 to 1993: spending on public education (K-12) increased by forty-seven percent, school enrollment declined by seven percent, and SAT scores declined by thirty-five points.

They further reported that: In 1993, none of the five states with the highest teacher's salaries was among the fifteen states with the top SAT scores; New Jersey had the highest per-pupil expenditure in the nation, and ranked thirty-ninth on SAT scores; North Dakota ranked forty-fourth in per-pupil expenditures but second in SAT scores and graduation rates; Utah ranked fifty-first in per-pupil expenditures, with the highest pupil-teacher ratio (23.8,) but ranked fourth in SAT scores; Washington, D.C. ranked fifth in per-pupil expenditures and has a lower pupil-teacher ratio than any state (11.9,) yet ranks forty-ninth in SAT scores and fiftieth in graduation rates.

More money clearly is not the answer to improving education effectiveness. Yet, anyone involved with the responsibility to improve education effectiveness always begs that more money is needed to improve education. Money is always a quick and convenient answer, because more money always creates a larger power source or an improved financial base for someone hiding in the education jungle.

Perhaps, as that 1966 research document suggests, education needs enough funding to provide reasonable and adequate opportunity.

Funding beyond that level should be for an unusual event, unless we have excess tax dollars we don't need for something else...or unless the purpose for education is for something other than to have more educated students.

Perhaps the purpose for schools might be other than student education. Even when that survey was conducted, in 1966, strong evidence suggested that education, even then, was less oriented to education needs than to political or economic factors. Those same suggestions and implications still exist even today, over thirty years later.

God bless America.

37

Families and Education

Few, if any, of our educational policies are targeted directly at improving education effectiveness. They appear to be more targeted toward political, social, and economic considerations. This is suggested by the idea that we have an education system, but we don't know what that system is designed to do. It's a vague concept. A vague concept is bound to create confusion and controversy, and those conditions create the need for political manipulation.

To summarize, over thirty years ago the most comprehensive education survey was conducted by researchers trying to prove that integration of schools would improve education success of black students. This survey, the *Equal Education Opportunity Survey,* was directed by the Johnson administration, in 1965. The *EEOS* failed to validate the idea that integration improved education effectiveness for black students. However, the survey did make several important findings. Those findings were never greatly publicized for two reasons: the volume of the survey was so large that it was difficult to interpret, and the conclusions did not prove the original hypothesis for the survey.

However, two important conclusions were made from that survey. One was that as long as a school provided the basic essentials necessary to provide education for a community, excess funding or excess opportunity did not help improve the grades or the effectiveness of those students. The other major conclusion was that: *schools make no difference - families make the difference,* regarding the quality of education for each individual student.

Fundamentally, the survey revealed that a child reared in a successful and learning family environment will be more receptive to learning, and will more likely anticipate personal success. Children reared in deprived family environments will be less likely to anticipate success, and are less likely to understand the relationship between education and personal success. They perceive no logical reason to work hard for an education that will serve them no good purpose.

This report formed no conclusions to present recommendations, for apparently none were found regarding the value and purpose of education; and the output gained from the amount of dollars input. Some other interesting ideas were formulated from that report, however, that influence the way we might view the education process. For example:

1. Most evidence indicated that increasing the amount of money

for education does not result in a better or higher educated person. There are diminishing returns on expenditures, for there's an optimum point at which any extra amount of money that's spent into the education system produces fewer results. Money is not necessarily the answer to better education.

2. There's no clear consensus to define a better education, or the purpose and use of an education. An education is not essential to train for most jobs; however, those jobs are inaccessible without specific educational levels.

3. High schools are not designed to prepare a person for a job, only to provide a minimum level of academic and social literacy. Rhetorical emphasis on job preparation creates confusion and ambivalence.

4. Schools and the education system are only alternative sources of redistributing wealth. It serves the same function as other welfare and social expenditures - not because it prepares students equally for economic success - but because it provides a comfortable physical facility that children from all the social classes may equally enjoy while they are there.

5. Survey results indicated that school desegregation caused more harm, educationally, to minority children. (This finding was the basic reason this massive research project was never publicized - it was contradictory to the purpose for the research.)

Why is this information important? The purpose for this analysis is to offer information and encouragement to students and their parents to help them make unemotional decisions concerning school, grades, and quality of education. According to this analysis, the family influence: principles, values, history, cultural background, and social standing has more influence on a student's success than does the difference between a grade of A, B, C or the school one attends.

What's the Real Education Status?

Students might be getting better educations than they or their parents think. Perhaps those educations aren't used because they are thought to be inferior. Recent events, particularly political and pseudo-intellectual rhetoric, have occurred to stress and politicize the education question. The plea for better education doesn't invite prudent questioning.

A rational politician or a self focused intellectual would be at a disadvantage by ignoring the great education dilemma of society. It's politically and socially dangerous to argue for rationality in the education question. One who would argue against improving the education system (spending more money on education) would be regarded as an uninspired and unpatriotic person. That person would be assumed to dislike his or her mother - and hate apple pie.

The *EEOS* report poses other realistic and current questions regarding education. These questions must be considered to determine if the education system has remained the same, has worsened, has been politicized or has merely been evaluated by a new set of perspectives by those doing the evaluation. Before these answers may be determined, however, some questions must be considered. They include:

What's the fundamental purpose for education?
What are the desired results of education?
Who should be educated - to which level?
Who is responsible for education?
What is needed to improve education?
Can the results be measured - how?

The social question hasn't been answered regarding the purpose of an education for an individual. As suggested earlier, society considers four possible reasons:

1. To develop basic social literacy.
2. To prepare a person for career opportunities.
3. To redistribute national wealth.
4. To control labor input.

God bless America.

38

Drones In 2025

My new book, Death Drones 2025, is much more than a fictional action adventure/thriller. Although it has much detailed information about how futuristic drones might work, including a hybrid drone lifted with helium and propelled by solar powered internal propellers, that's only part of the story. Families torn apart by a tyrannical government, and survival in the wilderness are the other two major parts of this story.

Death Drones describes two futuristic drones. (Or are they futurist?) One is a large mother drone that carries four smaller drones for search and kill missions. The mother drone replenishes power for the smaller drones so they can remain over an area for a long period searching in forests or any terrain. They are lightly armed for their missions. The other major drone is armed with a death ray that strikes without warning from the sky. Both major drones are camouflaged. The surprise in the story concerns their method of camouflage.

Just as in Nazi Germany, words spoken within families and between people are monitored. Any criticism against the government results in a person disappearing. If one in a family is targeted, the others are also targeted. In this story, Janice desperately searches for her two sons who disappeared because they made remarks against the government in school. Her husband had already been the target of the death ray. Since this is now a cashless society, all unusual purchases are monitored at the Data Hub in Utah. Buy three shovels at the same time, and a death drone appears to greet you.

This book also has many ideas for wilderness survival. Some are based on my childhood experiences in central Mississippi, and others by research. Personal experiences I included in the book are: how to catch crawfish in a shallow creek, how to identify and shell hickory nuts and black walnuts, how to find edible acorns, and how to find fish bait anywhere. I was surprised to learn how many edible wild plants there are from my research in a book, 'The Forager's Harvest,' by Samuel Thayer. Did you know cattails and canna lily, among many others, are edible? There are also many berries and fruit in the wild.

Hopefully, we will never have to be concerned about these things - but I wouldn't bet my life on it. The first survival items I bought were fish hooks, fishing line, much twine, and a good knife. The next was everstrike matches. Why twine? For tying things together to make a shelter. Basic preparation for emergencies is not really that expensive. Who knows ......?

God bless America.

39

Arming the Postal Department

The weapons build-up by our government continues. Why?

The link below includes the following information:

"On Jan. 31, the USPS Supplies and Services Purchasing Office posted a notice on the Federal Business Opportunities website asking contractors to register with USPS as potential ammunition suppliers for a variety of cartridges."

"While the government gears up for civil unrest and stockpiles ammo without limit, private gun owners on the other hand are finding ammunition shelves empty at gun stores across America, including shortages of once-common cartridges such as .22 Long Rifle." (In my recently released novel: Death Drones 2025, I included this information about lack of .22 Long Rifle ammunition.)

Now, they are accumulating more than two billion rounds of ammunition, including hollow point.

I've mentioned this before, but I think it's worthy of a reminder many more times before the end of Obama's administration - if there will be an end to Obama's administration. This reminder is regarding the purchase of 1.6 billion rounds of ammunition by the

Obama administration. That's not a typo - it's real - BILLION. Why? According to those who have current knowledge that's equivalent to enough ammunition to fight the war in Afghanistan for seven more years - yes, SEVEN years.

When questioned, the answer given was 'for training purposes.' But, why would anyone use half a million rounds of hollow-point ammunition for training? Hollow-point bullets are used only when deadly force is intended - never ever for training. They are more expensive - and they shatter on impact.

Recently I read an article that suggested the Obama administration was trying a back-door approach to gun control. Consuming all the available ammunition on the market, and planned to be on the market, would, in effect, create the same result as strict gun control. What good is a gun without bullets? Obama's actions to control guns create two important questions. Why is he afraid for American citizens to be armed? What might happen if ammunition is not available on the regular market for American citizens?

Why is Obama afraid for American citizens to be armed?

Would Obama be afraid for American citizens to be armed if he didn't have something in mind that would cause American citizens to be concerned about his plans or his actions for or against America? What makes him think citizens would feel a need to be armed? Is it for the reason our Founding Fathers, in the Constitution, allowed citizens to arm themselves. That purpose was to oppose tyranny and despotism.

This is the link for more information regarding this new action by the Postal Department - perhaps now a new member of Homeland Security.

http://www.infowars.com/u-s-postal-service-announces-giant-ammo-purchase/

God bless America.

40

Obama and Alinsky

This morning, I listened to Obama's answer (non answer) to Bill O'Reilly's question: "Did Secretary Panetta tell you the Benghazi attack was by terrorists?" Obama refused to answer the question and ducked and dodged all around it. He spoke in otherisms, even after he was prodded three times to answer. His action and comments immediately reminded me of that Saul Alinsky thing again. I'll repeat it here as a reminder of his deceit.

This is how Bestofluck.com describes Saul Alinsky's '12 Rules for Radicals.' They are:

RULE 1: "Power is not only what you have, but what the enemy thinks you have." Power is derived from 2 main sources – money and people. Have-Nots must build power from flesh and blood. (These are two things of which there is a plentiful supply. Government and corporations always have a difficult time appealing to people, and usually do so almost exclusively with economic arguments.)

RULE 2: "Never go outside the expertise of your people." It results in confusion, fear and retreat. Feeling secure adds to the backbone of anyone. (Organizations under attack wonder why radicals don't address the "real" issues. This is why. They avoid things with which they have no knowledge.)

RULE 3: "Whenever possible, go outside the expertise of the enemy." Look for ways to increase insecurity, anxiety and uncertainty. (This happens all the time. Watch how many organizations under attack are blind-sided by seemingly irrelevant arguments that they are then forced to address.)

RULE 4: "Make the enemy live up to its own book of rules." If the rule is that every letter gets a reply, send 30,000 letters. You can kill them with this because no one can possibly obey all of their own rules. (This is a serious rule. The besieged entity's very credibility and reputation is at stake, because if activists catch it lying or not living up to its commitments, they can continue to chip away at the damage.)

RULE 5: "Ridicule is man's most potent weapon." There is no defense. It's irrational. It's infuriating. It also works as a key pressure point to force the enemy into concessions. (Pretty crude, rude and mean, huh? They want to create anger and fear.)

RULE 6: "A good tactic is one your people enjoy." They'll keep doing it without urging and come back to do more. They're doing their thing, and will even suggest better ones. (Radical activists, in this sense, are no different than any other human being. We all avoid "un-fun" activities, and but we revel at and enjoy the ones that work and bring results.)

RULE 7: "A tactic that drags on too long becomes a drag." Don't become old news. (Even radical activists get bored. So to keep them excited and involved, organizers are constantly coming up with new tactics.)

RULE 8: "Keep the pressure on. Never let up." Keep trying new things to keep the opposition off balance. As the opposition masters one approach, hit them from the flank with something new. (Attack, attack, attack from all sides, never giving the reeling organization a chance to rest, regroup, recover and re-strategize.)

RULE 9: "The threat is usually more terrifying than the thing itself." Imagination and ego can dream up many more consequences than any activist. (Perception is reality. Large organizations always prepare a worst-case scenario, something that may be furthest from the activists' minds. The upshot is that the organization will expend enormous time and energy, creating in its own collective mind the direst of conclusions. The possibilities can easily poison the mind and result in demoralization.)

RULE 10: "If you push a negative hard enough, it will push through and become a positive." Violence from the other side can win the public to your side because the public sympathizes with the underdog. (Unions used this tactic. Peaceful [albeit loud] demonstrations during the heyday of unions in the early to mid-20th Century incurred management's wrath, often in the form of violence that eventually brought public sympathy to their side.)

RULE 11: "The price of a successful attack is a constructive alternative." Never let the enemy score points because you're caught without a solution to the problem. (Old saw: If you're not part of the solution, you're part of the problem. Activist organizations have an agenda, and their strategy is to hold a place at the table, to be given a forum to wield their power. So, they have to have a compromise solution.)

RULE 12: Pick the target, freeze it, personalize it, and polarize it." Cut off the support network and isolate the target from sympathy. Go after people and not institutions; people hurt faster than institutions. (This is cruel, but very effective. Direct, personalized criticism and ridicule works.)

To understand how Obama, Harry Reid, and others of their ilk are using these tactics, and why they are so effective, just listen to their words as they speak them. Then associate those surprise, aggressive, attack, and far-out charges to these 12 rules. The next time you hear Obama speak, listen closely to his highly-charged words. (And in this case listen to how he avoids an answer and places the blame on someone else - in this case FOX News.)

God bless America.

41
A Plan to Waste More Tax Dollars

So the president plans to promote more early education - Pre-K. This is another plan to waste more tax money.

There's a great fallacy when considering education. Only one part is considered - education opportunity. There are two other parts: cultural programming and personal motivation. These are never considered. Those who promote education programs assume more opportunity, alone, will improve education.

Providing more opportunity (money) is like pouring water into a quart jar. A quart jar holds only a quart of water. Pouring a gallon of water into a quart jar will result in three quarts being wasted. The same is true with education opportunity. Until the receptor is prepared to receive what's input, all the extra will be wasted - more taxes spent without education improvement.

That receptor, students, can be prepared to receive more opportunity in only two ways. First, the child's family culture must demonstrate the value of education. Second, the child must understand why education is a needed value, to fulfill his or her immediate needs - not some unfelt future need. For example, at age five a child is not influenced (motivated) to prepare for a job.

Research shows early education has no effect on education effectiveness beyond the third grade. James Coleman, in his 1966 EEOS Report, explained it clearly, "Schools make little difference; families make the difference." Coleman's survey included 3000 schools and 600,000 students and teachers. The Johnson administration, who commissioned the survey, disregarded his findings and conclusions. It's been ignored ever since. The result has been drop-outs - a continuous and predictable 30 percent. Some school districts in inner cities - even more than 75 percent.

Instead of focusing on earlier and earlier education (some propose to take it to age 1) we must focus on eliminating drop-outs. We must give students an option (probably in the 9th grade) to advance academically or vocationally. Why should weak academic students be forced to compete with those preparing for college?

Drop-outs are our education problem, not grades. Over 90 percent of those in jail or prison are school drop-outs. Let's give kids a chance, not force them to leave school because they know they can't compete and they become embarrassed. Who wants to live in a hellish environment?

My book, 'The Education Jungle,' explains much more.

God bless America.

42

Should You Have Guns?

The following article was passed around in an email. I don't remember who wrote this article, but it exposed a serious situation created by the Obama administration:

"Do you have a gun in your House? When I had my gangrene gallbladder taken out and spent 10 days in the hospital for what should have been an overnight stay the insurance company kicked me out. I had home nurse visits for two weeks and was asked if I had guns in the house. I respond that if I did I would not tell them. So the below has some merit. FYI, I am passing this along...there are comments from two other people that have also been asked if they keep guns in the house. The nurse just kind of slipped it in along with all the other regular questions. I told her I refused to answer because it was against the law to ask.

Everyone, whether you have guns or not, should give a neutral answer so they have no idea who does and who doesn't. My doctor asked me if I had guns in my house and also if any were loaded. I, of course, answered yes to both questions. Then he asked why I kept a loaded gun close to my bed. I answered that my son, who is a certified gun instructor and also works for Homeland Security, advised me that an unloaded, locked up gun is no protection against criminal attack. The Government now requires these questions be asked of people on Medicare, and probably everyone else. Just passing this along for your information: I had to visit a doctor other than my regular doctor when my doctor was on vacation. One of the questions on the form I had to fill out was: Do you have any guns in your house? My answer was None of your business!! So it is out there! It is either an insurance issue or government intervention.

Either way, it is out there and the second the government gets into your medical records (as they want to under Obamacare) it will become a major issue and will ultimately result in lock and load!!

Please pass this on to all the other retired guys and gun owners. Thanks, from a Vietnam Vet and retired Police Officer: I had a doctors appointment at the local VA clinic yesterday and found out something very interesting that I would like to pass along. While going through triage before seeing the doctor, I was asked at the end of the exam, three questions: 1. Did I feel stressed? 2. Did I feel threatened? 3. Did I feel like doing harm to someone? The nurse then informed me, that if I had answered yes to any of the questions, I would have lost my concealed carry permit as it would have gone into my medical records and the VA would have reported it to Homeland Security.

Looks like they are going after the vets first. Other gun people like retired law enforcement will probably be next. Then when they go after the civilians, what argument will they have? Be forewarned and be aware. The Obama administration has gone on record as considering veterans and gun owners potential terrorists. Whether you are a gun owner, veteran or not, YOU"VE BEEN WARNED ! If you know veterans and gun owners, please pass this on to them. Be very cautious about what you say and to whom!!"

43

Points of View

Finally - finished the draft of 'Death Drones 2025' at 102,000 words. Now I'm half through the first edit. As I approach the half-way point of the edit, I was thinking how this book fits in with my other two political action-adventure books: 'America 20XX' and '666: Mark of the Beast.' As I'm editing I realize a major difference.

'America 20XX' gives events happening only in the United States, and as I wrote previously, gives points of view from both the antagonist and the protagonist. In retrospect, that seems to focus more on events, situations, and conclusions. It's a story about what's happening. (If you haven't picked up on it, the XX refers to a year - you can imagine your own last two digits which represent a year. Many of us believe that year is very soon.)

'666' is similar, but it encompasses a wider perspective and a broader war, worldwide, particularly in the middle-east and Israel. It also gives points of view from both perspectives, protagonist and antagonist. The last major scene in this story is the conclusion of the 'Battle of Armageddon.' This last scene holds the surprise, and focuses more on that conclusion than on the problems of a specific protagonist. (Many people also believe the time of this scene could be very near.)

'Death Drones 2025' has many survival scenes other than

defending against fierce 'Devil' drones. It's also filled with examples of how to survive in the wilderness. I used many of my personal experiences growing up in the woods in central Mississippi for the background of these examples, for example how to catch crawfish in a shallow stream; and how to identify other edibles, including snakes. While editing this book, I realize that viewing from one perspective seems to create more suspense, and more concern about specific individuals or families.

Obviously, points of view are very important, depending on the purpose of the writing. I enjoy writing both. Have fun.

God bless America.

44
A Kingly President

Almost there! Just reached 96,000 words - 4000 words to go. Maybe I can finish the draft in 3 or 4 more days. Then of course comes the editing and final formatting. My wife has already started the first editing part. I'm still aiming for self-publishing in February.

For this book and all my other novels, I never know exactly where it's going when I begin. I just set a beginning situation then let the minor plots and characters develop themselves from there. My two guiding themes were a tyrannical government gone wild, and different drones used in unusual ways as a major tool of that tyrannical government. A president that pushed the Constitution farther and farther, until it faded into obsolete and irrelevant history.

As the book developed, of course my strong political leanings took over. The president, in this story, developed such a strong voting block that his words became power. Anything he wanted and demanded he got, because his opposition had no influence. From his personal ambition, and the full support of his 'bought' supporters, he proclaimed himself as king. No one could challenge him or stop him. Doesn't this sound eerily similar to events taking place today?

(6:00: Just had to take a quick break to put out my bird feeders behind my house, near some woods. If I leave them out overnight, two raccoons climb the thin metal poles and pull them down. I have solar flood lights there so I can watch them every night. I always leave some bird seed for them.)

With that power, he proclaimed traditional citizens who supported the basic Constitution as terrorists - and unleashed war against them. When neighbors and fellow citizens refused to carry out the worst atrocities against their fellow citizens, he recruited 'Others' from foreign nations to perform those tasks. Political cleansing? Moral cleansing? Religious cleansing? I'm not sure.

The major difference in this novel and my others is in point of view. Previously, I gave points of view from both sides, antagonist and protagonist. In this the point of view is from only those being persecuted. Most takes place within a group trying to survive after they barely escape with their lives.

I'm not sure of the ending. I haven't got there yet, but have already set the stage for it.

God bless America.

45

Something Is Interfering With My Program

Is it my imagination? I have a graphics package by Broderbund (ClickArt 300,000) that I've used for over 15 years. It's the graphics program I used to make the covers for all my books, especially those that likely are offensive to Obama and his followers. All of a sudden, just tonight, they refuse to process on my computer. Fortunately, I completed the cover for, 'Death Drones 2025' before this happened. Hopefully, it will be my last book because I need to catch more fish and improve my golf game before age forces me to learn how to play solitaire and bridge.

Is it just my imagination? Fortunately, I also have a hobby of building and repairing old computers and computer parts. Stuck back in one of my closets are other laptops and desktop computers. When my program refused to operate on my active computer hooked to the internet, I tried it on one was not hooked up to the internet. Guess what? It worked perfectly. I tried it on another computer hooked to the internet. Guess what? It didn't work.

Now, I'm not one to get paranoid, but with all my anti-Obama blogs and writings, I'm not surprised something like this happened. Just as a joke, I think, every time a helicopter passes over our house, my wife tells me to duck. I'm not paranoid, but I do watch for any unusual packages or noises that occur around my house, especially at night.

It was a total shock that my graphics program stopped working just a few minutes ago on my active computer. But, I have others to help me do what I need to do. Maybe I'll be forced to write more Obama books if the purpose is to challenge me. Gosh! Darn! Heck!

God bless America.

46

What to Do

Gosh! Darn! Heck! I forgot I had started a novel, 'Escape From Troy,' when I stopped it to write, 'King Obama: America's Greatest Danger.' At that time I felt that non-fiction information was more important than a novel. When I finished that 'King Obama' book I became focused on the danger of future drones. Now that I'm almost finished with that one, I just discovered the beginning of the forgotten 'Troy' book.

And I promised myself 'Drones' would be my last book. I said I needed to improve my golf game and catch more largemouth bass in the Pearl River.

Oh, well. What does one do? No one wants to discard the beginnings of a new book, especially a historical novel that ends up in a place like Ephesus, in Turkey. Much important Roman, Greek, Ionian, Islamic and Biblical history occurred there. I guess

I'll have to take it on when my current one is finished. But, what about my golf game and all those fish waiting for me!

The history of Ephesus is more interesting than one might imagine. It's the home of many of the people named in the Bible, including Mary, and John, who wrote the Book of Revelation while on Patmos, just off the coast of Ephesus. The ancient city of Troy is not far from Ephesus. It's near the modern city of Istanbul. Click this link if you would like to discover more very interesting things about Ephesus.

http://www.ephesus.us/

47

Fiction or Reality

I'm taking a little break from writing this evening. It's not just to celebrate reaching 75,000 words of 100,000 words planned for my novel, it's also to allow my subconscious to catch up and plan the next scenes and events. I'm sure I'll be back at it tomorrow with a goal of finishing the draft by the end of January, and completing the editing by the end of February. Hopefully, my wife will start the editing now before I finish the draft.

I never outline a novel when I write. I just create an action scene, the more violent the scene, the more intense I plan the story to evolve. This novel, 'Death Drones 2025,' begins with three men preparing their survival camp being killed with a death ray from the sky, unseen. The other members of the group then know they must make different plans to survive. Unknown to the survival planners, the government has developed drones with different capabilities and different missions. I haven't got to this part yet, but shortly I will write about unmanned drones being guided by government loyalists in a central location because the government has become suspicious about the loyalty of pilots of manned aircraft.

Just imagine hundreds of drones armed with different capabilities for different missions. For example, a large drone could fly over a wooded or camouflaged area and release poison gases to eliminate everyone hiding there. A small quiet drone supported by a gas bubble and propelled with either small propellers or jets, guided by infrared or heat devices, could stalk a target in the woods at night and fire a tiny poison dart at that person. He would never hear or see it coming. And, what about a mother drone permanently parked above a suspect area. It could remain in place indefinitely from a combination of gas and solar energy. Consider the inhuman possibilities of these 'drones from Hell.'

Who would do such a thing? Who would be so cruel and ruthless? One person comes quickly to mind. He's the one often mentioned in the Bible Book of Revelation. This reference guides much of my story, beginning with the woman being driven to the hills (Christians going into hiding because of persecution.) Although the Bible reference doesn't drive the story, I present enough implications that anyone who understands Revelation will catch frequent glimpses of these implications.

Is a concept such as this even conceivable? Why has our current government started stockpiling weapons, armor, and billions of rounds of ammunition? Why is our government beginning to imply that many of our veterans returning from foreign wars are subject to persuasion by domestic terror groups?

Is this far-fetched scenario of which I'm writing even conceivable? You bet your life it is. Just keep up with, and closely analyze things happening already.

God bless America.

48

Total Control of Our Lives

In my Dec. 31st blog I asked the question: "What if our new healthcare program eventually required one to have a microchip installed to monitor everyone's health status? What possibilities would that present for a tyrannical government?"

With our advancing technology, growing populations, increasing health care costs, more intrusion and demands by our government into health care responsibility, and growing wireless interaction with heart pump patients, is there any doubt that soon microchip implants will be used that will allow a super computer (the massive NSA Data Hub in Utah) to monitor the basics such as blood pressure and heart rates? It's not beyond technological reason to imagine a microchip could do the same process as a full blood and urine analysis that now is performed at hospital and clinical laboratories. Wouldn't this be more logical than the way these analyses are currently done? And, with fast-advancing technology, I suspect we have that capability now.

The defining factor would be cooperation among all the agencies involved. Since the government is fast taking over complete control of health care, this cooperation will fast become less important. They will just do it. In that same blog I also stated, "If they can think of it they will do it." Doesn't that system sound really logical?

But, what are the dangers? Just use your imagination to consider what a tyrannical government could do with that capability. Or even a rogue administrator who had a grudge against a person or a community, or an organization. The possibilities are endless. If you don't believe how much capability the government, especially the NSA, now has just click on the link to find out. And, their capability is rapidly expanding.

http://www.foreignpolicy.com/articles/2013/10/15/the_nsa_s_new_codebreakers

Do we really want our government involved in our health care system? I think not. Read the excerpt on the information page of my upcoming book, 'Death Drones 2025.' It gives just one example of the many possibilities. When the government controls our health care - they control our lives TOTALLY!

God bless America.

49

Hacking At the Data Hub

Do you remember this comment from my blog on Dec. 31, 'Stress and the Data Hub?' (Don't forget: if you build it they will come;

if they can think of it they will do it; if they have the capability they will not disregard that opportunity.)

I was surprised just one day later by an article that appeared in my local newspaper that supports the fundamental concepts of my quote above:

"LONDON - Apple Inc. Says it played no role in the NSA's alleged efforts to hack their iPhone, explaining that it was unaware of a recently revealed program apparently aimed at turning the best-selling smart-phone into an improvised listening device."

So — I did a little more research and found the following information. It was reported by someone named 'Kelly' on google on Dec. 30:

"The NSA allegedly has a back door into iOS that allows the agency to intercept text messages, address book entries and more, says a report on The Daily Dot. This snooping uses encryption to hide the data that is being sent back to the NSA and is done covertly to avoid detection.

The NSA spyware was unveiled by security researcher Jacob Appelbaum, who was speaking at the Chaos Communication Conference in Hamburg, Germany. According to Applebaum, the NSA developed a program called DROPOUTJEEP as implant on a user's phone. The app is manually installed on a device via a shipment rerouting program that allows the NSA to grab select packages and pass them through their facilities before they land in the hands of the consumer. These details are contained in a 2008 NSA document leaked by Appelbaum.

The DROPOUTJEEP app can push/pull files from a device, download SMS messages, get location data, turn on the mic/camera and more. The system allegedly has a "100 percent success rate when it comes to implanting iOS devices with spyware."

Whether Apple has provided the NSA with a backdoor into iOS is not known. Applebaum hints that either Apple sabotaged iOS or that the NSA knows about exploits that work against Apple products. "Do you think Apple helped them with that?" Appelbaum asked. "I hope Apple will clarify that."

In the past, Apple has vehemently denied working with the NSA to spy on its customers. The company, along with seven other technology customers, has sent an open letter to the President and Congress asking Washington to change its government surveillance practices worldwide. You can watch Applebaum's presentation below and sound off in the comments about this latest NSA program." End of Article.

http://www.iphonehacks.com/2013/12/leaked-documents-details-nsa-can-spy-ios-owners.html

"If they think of it they will do it." Perhaps I should tone down some of the futuristic scenes in my upcoming novel: Death Drones 2025. It's now at 71,000 words and on schedule for a February release.

God bless America.

50

Stress at The Data Hub

An interesting thought occurred after I wrote my last blog regarding blogs, terrorists, and stress. It's my understanding that all our personal information recorded at the IRS and soon our healthcare status under the new governmental controlled healthcare system will be merged into the new Data Hub center in Utah. It's a new center that has the capacity to store information about every person on earth for twenty years. It's also the center that stores the information the NSA now has about every U.S. citizen. Clearly, all this information about every citizen is now merged in one place - the NSA Data Hub in Utah. This situation has very deep, dark, and dire possibilities to control the future of every American.

For example, how easy would it be for the government to annotate 'stressed' on a person's health record. That would be an automatic cue for anyone performing a background check for a gun sale to refuse that sale. The annotation of 'stress' would mean that person (you and I) might be considered unstable. Who could stop the Department of Homeland Security from making that entry on one's health record? According to reports, the VA already has a question regarding 'stress' on visits now.

As a veteran, I was asked about 'stress' during my recent visit last month. Really - no lie. Since I laughed at that question and replied, "Are you kidding me?" I think I passed that stress test. But, with all these comments I have been submitting, who knows what will be entered on my record in the future?

The government now controls everything and can do what they please - almost without recourse. One more Obama appointee to the Supreme Court would make Obama and his administration untouchable. They would have a free run at whatever they wanted to do. Gun control legislation would be unnecessary. They could control gun sales with just one annotation on a health record - 'stress.'

And, what about a credit check for a home loan. What would keep the government from linking all that information together at the Data Hub. (Don't forget: if you build it they will come; if they can think of it they will do it; if they have the capability they will not disregard that opportunity.) Limiting one's opportunity to get a loan to buy a house in a certain area would change the opportunity and freedom we expect as Americans. That opportunity could easily be used by the government to control demographic diversity by race, ethnicity, or economic status. Would our government do it - would they go that far? You bet your life Obama and his administration would. Some way they would do it in the name of fighting terrorism and creating diversity. Just one little word - 'stress.'

Can Barack Hussein Obama be trusted to support and follow the guidelines of our U.S. Constitution? Can any man who spews as many lies and falsehoods from his lips as Obama be trusted at all - especially in anything that concerns honor and fidelity?

My next blog will be related to this one. What if our new healthcare program eventually required one to have a microchip installed to monitor everyone's health status? What possibilities would that present for a tyrannical government?

God bless America.

51

The Terrorists Are Coming

Why am I taking so much of my valuable time writing a book about the danger of drones? Because I believe drones will become a powerful threat against American citizens, and many others throughout the world, in the next few years; and reaching its ultimate tyranny in the year 2025.

I still haven't settled on a title. At the moment, at 70,000 words of 100,000 planned, the title is, 'Death Drones 2025.' I have also considered other titles for connected reasons. One consideration is, 'Fire From the Sky.' This is a biblical reference from Revelation that says the False Prophet, the Antichrist's great supporter, will create miracles such as sending fire from the sky, to convince people to worship the Antichrist. Another possible title is, 'Antichrist Drones.' From my many previous blogs it's pretty clear what this title might represent. I don't think I have to spell it out any further.

Why do I think death drones will be a tolerated part of American life in the near future? Because of the word, "Terrorist." A government in power has the power to declare anyone who poses a threat, especially to themselves, as terrorists. As citizens, we automatically interpret any 'terrorist' as a threat. Perhaps anyone defending themselves against tyranny might be labeled as a terrorist by the government. (Consider the Ruby Ridge and the David Koresh Dividians events as examples. The government never explained why all those people were killed.)

Already, some in government have claimed that many military veterans returning from middle-east wars are vulnerable to be drawn into 'terrorist' organizations. Many of these are already being excluded from buying personal defensive handguns if they are identified by the government as suffering from 'stress.' How far will they take this classification of 'stress?' How freely will the 'terrorist' label be applied?

Regarding the Antichrist: minor antichrists do exist at this time, but they are not The Antichrist. According to scripture, The Antichrist (the beast) will arise when the seven continents are controlled by one government. We are not there yet, but the word 'Terrorism' might eventually cause that to happen. My book, '666: Mark of the Beast,' covers that time period and that event.

I've got to get this darn book finished. I will be 75 on Jan. 19, and there are too many golf balls left to be hit, and too many bass left to be caught in the Pearl River, north of New Orleans. This will be my last book - but I said that after my last book. Oh, well.

God bless America.

52

Christians Are Being Slaughtered

This is the continuation of my blog from yesterday explaining the dynamic war on Christianity, in America and worldwide. Christians are being slaughtered everywhere. Perhaps this might explain why. It's from Revelation.

This review by Propheysysigns.com is taken from Revelation 12: 17. It's #16 of 20 prophesy signs.

Reference: "Then the dragon was enraged at the woman and went off to make war against the rest of her offspring--those who obey God's commandments and hold to the testimony of Jesus Christ.

What it looks like:

Throughout history, Satan, the Dragon, has abused mankind, and specifically the Woman, the nation Israel, in an attempt to kill the Messiah. During the End Times, this persecution will intensify, and Satan will become laser-focused in his final persecution of the Woman and her final offspring, the Church. These verses clearly teach the Church will endure the Great Tribulation. Why does God allow this attack upon His Bride? As He has throughout the history of the Church, God allows persecution and suffering in our lives in order to purify believers and make the Church stronger.

The Church and Israel will have a difficult time during the reign of terror of the Antichrist and the False Prophet. All out spiritual war commences when Satan will be cast out of heaven to this earth. We will be called to remain patient during this 3 ½ year period, which is a relatively short time. We are called to be faithful, keep his commandments and some will have the high privilege of being martyrs as they hold to their testimony of Jesus during the Great Tribulation." End of reference.

There are three other critical references in this event. First is Revelation 12: 6. "And the woman fled into the wilderness, where she hath a place prepared of God, that they should feed her there a thousand two hundred and threescore days." Perhaps this means Christians must go into hiding until the tribulation passes - a time when many Christians will be killed - beheaded. The second related reference is Revelation 20: 4:

"...and I saw the souls of them that were beheaded for the witness of Jesus, and for the word of God, and which had not worshiped the beast, neither his image, neither had received his mark upon their foreheads , or in their hands; and they lived and reigned with Christ a thousand years." (This is the quote often used as the basis of the 'Rapture.' According to this reference only these will be included - not every Christian at that time. The third related reference is Revelation 13: 17:

"And that no man might buy or sell, save he that had the mark, or the name of the beast, or the number of his name." Does this not clearly mean we are fast moving to a cashless society? That way, every person can be totally controlled by a single authority. These are the major references that form the basis of my upcoming novel: 'Death Drones 2025.'

God bless America.

53

Obama Supports the Muslim Brotherhood

I was listening to news this morning and heard a report about three churches being attacked and bombed in Baghdad, and other Christians still being intimidated and slaughtered throughout other Muslim countries. And, all this keeps happening and intensifying - without any retort from our State Department or Barack Hussein Obama. In my inquisitiveness, I researched 'Obama and the Muslim Brotherhood.' These are the first two articles that appeared. They are from the site, Atlas Shrugs, by Pamela Geller:

"Oct 31: Obama Homeland Security advisor Mohamed Elibiary: "United States of America Is An Islamic Country." Homeland Security unmosqued.

Obama appointee, Homeland Security Advisory Council member and Muslim Brotherhood supporter Mohamed Elibiary is a Muslim Brotherhood zealot actively promoting the Islamic supremacist agenda. He used his new federal security clearance to access a sensitive database and download state and local intelligence reports on the Texas Department of Public Safety and sell them to mainstream media outlets to smear Texas Gov. Rick Perry as an islamophobe and racist. Instead of being fired at the time, Elibiary was just given .... a promotion.

Despite exposing these Muslim Brotherhood operatives at Atlas as early as 2010 here (even an Egyptian magazine did a bombshell article on Muslim Brotherhood infiltration in the Obama administration in January 2013 as well), the Obama administration continued to appoint enemy operatives to key posts.

Muslim Brotherhood operatives have direct access to the White House. Arif Alikhan, assistant secretary of Homeland Security for policy development; Mohammed Elibiary, a member of the Homeland Security Advisory Council; Rashad Hussain, the U.S. special envoy to the Organization of the Islamic Conference; Salam al-Marayati, co-founder of the Muslim Public Affairs Council (MPAC); Imam Mohamed Magid, president of the Islamic Society of North America (ISNA); and Eboo Patel, a member of President Obama's Advisory Council on Faith-Based Neighborhood Partnerships.

Dec 21: Obama's Partner Muslim Brotherhood Terror-Prez Morsi linked to al-Qaeda Chief.

I know it's Pravda, but the American press will never cover it. Obama is a huge supporter of the terrorist group the Muslim Brotherhood, and the US press is voluntary state-run media. Hence, no coverage. The recordings of these phone conversations will tell all.(Not available at this time.)

Before the "election," the Obama administration warned Egypt's military leaders to speedily hand over power to the Muslim Brotherhood or risk losing billions of dollars in U.S. military and economic aid to the country. And Obama scrambled to save Morsi when 33 million Egyptians marched to oust him (that was 22 million more than voted for the jihadist Egyptian prez).

Obama's unwavering support for the terrorist Muslim Brotherhood group is so unstinting that he punished the Egyptian people for throwing off the the Islamic yoke of tyranny. He suspended hundred of millions in military and other aid to punish the people of Egypt for throwing the Brotherhood out of power.Obama's support for the Muslim Brotherhood caused enormous anger in Egypt. Not only do we need to hear the recorded conversations between Morsi and Al Qaeda leader Muhammad Al-Zawahiri; we need to hear the conversations between Morsi and Obama." End of articles.

After I reviewed these articles and more, a major question zapped into my mind. That question: aren't Christians in our country - America - our great nation that was founded on principles based on Christianity - aren't we also under this same attack? The Obama administration, and many other organized subversive groups, are attacking Christianity while protecting all the Muslim foundations in our nation. Islam has already declared that, "America is a Muslim nation."

My next post will be a direct biblical reference to this activity. It's from Revelation.

God bless America.

54

Obama Encourages Abomination

Some people are not fully aware of the basis of the 'Duck Dynasty' controversy. The man from Duck Dynasty was probably speaking as he understood things, and as he was only intellectually capable of doing. In his own interpretation, he certainly made his point and brought forth what might be a 'below the surface' major controversy - especially between Christians and non-Christians.

As a Christian, I pass judgment on no person other than myself. My opinion of others is irrelevant, other than for choosing close friends. Judging myself to stay right in God's view is a full time job. And, as I believe, when final judgment does come, it's a very personal one-on-one situation. However, in my opinion, to express an opinion is also a one-on-one situation. That opinion expresses a belief which will in the end, also be judged by God. What right do we have to judge other people's opinions, and to become violent and oppressive against that person, as many have done against that Duck Dynasty man who expressed his opinion in relation to his interpretation of Bible references?

Speaking from the Bible, the man was absolutely correct. Here are two references that support his comments:

"Leviticus 18:22, "You shall not lie with a male as with a woman; it is an abomination."

"Leviticus 20:13, "If a man lies with a male as with a woman, both of them have committed an abomination."

Many sins encouraged by Satan, 'that old serpent,' are referenced in the Bible, but some are more clearly emphasized than others. Consider these and look around to see how often many of these are coming more commonplace in everyday life. These are many other things John wrote about as transgressions and fornication. According to the Bible, these things will also be magnified in the end times announcing the arrival of the Antichrist. Many of these 'abominations,' as expressed in the Bible, are also encouraged and promoted by Barack Hussein Obama, especially homosexuality, lying lips, and sowing discord:

Proverbs 6:6-19, "There are six things that the Lord hates, seven that are an abomination to him: haughty eyes, a lying tongue, and hands that shed innocent blood, a heart that devises wicked plans, feet that make haste to run to evil, a false witness who breathes out lies, and one who sows discord among brothers."

Galations 5:19-21, "Now the works of the flesh are evident: sexual immorality, impurity, sensuality, idolatry, sorcery, enmity, strife, jealousy, fits of anger, rivalries, dissensions, divisions, envy, drunkenness, orgies, and things like these. I warn you, as I warned you before, that those who do such things will not inherit the kingdom of God."

Romans 1:26-27, "For this reason God gave them up to dishonorable passions. For their women exchanged natural relations for those that are contrary to nature; and the men likewise gave up natural relations with women and were consumed with passion for one another, men committing shameless acts with men and receiving in themselves the due penalty for their error."

Proverbs 12:22, "Lying lips are an abomination to the Lord, but those who act faithfully are his delight."

Isaiah 49:1 "Listen to me, you islands; hear this, you distant nations: Before I was born the LORD called me; from my mother's womb he has spoken my name."

God bless America.

55

Republicans Must Stop Being Cowards

In my blog on 12-16, I evaluated Nancy Pelosi's comment that 'Republicans disrespect women.' I need not repeat that whole evaluation here since you can find it below this article. In that blog, I stated that Republicans must not be afraid, or too embarrassed, to use that same Alinsky approach. Democrats, especially Barack Obama, Nancy Pelosi, Harry Reid, David Axelrod, and others on the Obama team have used that Alinsky approach (attack and keep attacking to keep the opponent off balance) since Obama came on the scene. Obama even taught that technique during his 'community organizing' days. (Do the research if you doubt this.)

Pelosi's statement was meant to occupy Republican's time on defense, and to plant seeds of doubt in the minds of vulnerable women who would believe that statement without question - as Saul Alinsky taught. Republicans, on the other hand, have tried to compete with logic and explanation. Logic and sound explanations only work in a society of many open and inquisitive minds. In the political world that does not exist.

Most political minds are cast in steel, and are not easily changed to the other side, no matter how much logic is involved. If

Republicans are to compete, they must understand this and actually compete on the same low attack level as Democrats have, as of late - as of the beginnings of Barack Obama. But, how can Republicans allow themselves to compete in what they might perceive as low graces of themselves? They must realize, as the Democrats already have, that politics have sunk well below logic. Both parties must have an equal footing so the best will rise to the top to lead our great nation. Obama has thrown mud in what was a clear and respectable stream. It's now a mud fight - like it or not! The dirtiest fighter should not always be allowed to win. We need the best people to lead our nation.

For example, when Nancy Pelosi says, "Republicans disrespect women," it's a waste of time, and falling right into her trap, by trying to criticize her statement and defeat her words. An attack on her will prove her point. Instead, Republicans should proclaim, "Democrats really hate black people and poor people." This puts the defense back on the other side. And, that idea can be justified, very simply. Just explain that Democrats give black people and poor people just enough to make them feel they are getting something. Instead, they hate them because they give them just enough to keep them begging forever. They don't give them ideas and reasons to rise to higher levels, to find ways to personal success; to find that dream of really being somebody, someday. The Democrats only give them enough to buy their loyalty; they don't give them aspirations. So, Democrats really do hate black people and poor people.

Republican and Democrat candidates should compete on an equal playing field where all voters can see. An attack should never be one-sided. But, alas, do Republicans have the foresight and courage to play the Democrats' Saul Alinsky game? Maybe they will learn.

God bless America.

56

Reality Creates Fiction

Still working hard on that new novel tentatively titled, 'Dark Drones: 2025.' I'm at 62,000 words now, with 40,000 to go - Maybe February. Anyway, this is a little snippet of the book I typed just 2 minutes ago. The setting: Carl and Evelyn are trying to make their way back to the survival site from a scouting mission to plan a rescue attempt for a friend in prison. They are hiding out in a busy mall until dark. That's when they travel:

He shook Evelyn and quietly told her to wake up. As she stirred he told her not to open her eyes; not to look up. Then he asked, "Are you awake - do you understand?"

She briefly opened her eyes but upon understanding what Carl said quickly responded. Then she sat upright and asked, "What's happening?"

"I think we're being watched. Don't look up, or the camera might do an eye identity probe. I don't know if we're on record with a match."

"What do we do now?"

"Stay alive, if we can." Carl knew he shouldn't have said that, it just slipped out. He continued, "Maybe we can find some unmonitored places in here until it gets dark. Whatever we do, let's not let them see panic - appear normal."

"Let's get some coffee at the food court. That's pretty normal, especially since I just woke up."

"Thank God they still take cash for those small purchases, but don't know how much longer that will last. Once that changes the government will have us totally by the balls with no opportunity for any personal freedom. They'll own us."

Evelyn replied, "Just look at us now. Will there be any difference? Fear; Fear; it's everywhere already. Now we're nothing more than obedient cells of a zombi's body. We're no longer humans with free wills."

Evelyn waited at the little table while Carl got the coffee. As he sat down to join her, resisting the strong urge to look around, he responded to her last comment, "That's why we gotta keep trying. Some of us have to persevere to keep hope alive for humanity. We can't let humanity die without trying to do something. We might fail, but by God, we should never just follow along with evil."

"Most are following that pied piper of destruction, already. His lies became honey for those who chose to close their eyes. They became so dependent on his promises they rallied behind him when he decided to appoint himself king. The other branches of government were castrated with his overwhelming support by those who saw their opportunity for social equality without effort, and even more."

"We gotta make it back, Evelyn; we gotta get this done."

God bless America.

57

Things We Must Never Forget

This is an update on my promise to repeat these questions until we are given real American answers from Barack Obama and his administration.

Things We Must Never Forget Until We Know All the Answers:

BENGHAZI

Why were four Americans killed?

Where was Hillary Clinton while it was happening?

Where was Barack Obama while it was happening?

Why did they lie and blame the event on a video?

Why were rescuers on 'stand by' told to 'stand down?'

Why wasn't more security provided in that 'danger zone?'

FAST AND FURIOUS

Who authorized the operation?

Why did the operation continue after weapons were lost?

Why did the procedure have no procedure?

Why weren't tracking devices used?

Why did Eric Holder lie about it?

Why did Barack Obama block the investigation?

Why is Obama not concerned about that loss of life?

THE IRS SCANDAL

What was the highest level involved?

Who initiated it?

Why hasn't anyone been fired or reprimanded?

How can this happen in our 'America?'

Shouldn't every American be concerned about government targeting: freedom and security? If one side can do it, so can the other side!

If our government can target American citizens in one way what about another? For instance - deadly and silent drones? This example demonstrates a rogue government is capable of anything if left unchecked in the beginning. When drones attack American citizens (and they will eventually) it will be in the name of 'fighting terrorism.'

SEAL TEAM 6

On August 6, 2011, 30 Americans were killed when a helicopter was ambushed and shot down by the Taliban, in Afghanistan. Of those, 22 were members of Seal Team 6, the unit that recently had killed Osama bin Laden. It was learned afterward that the names of the 7 Afghans onboard did not match the names of those that were assigned to be onboard. Clearly, someone higher up knew what was about to happen and saved 7 of their Afghan friends - or sacrificed some other undesirables in their places.

It was our government who announced the fact that Bin Laden was killed by Seal Team 6, almost immediately after the event. So - who was responsible for their deaths? Questions have never even been asked about this event.

The first responsibility of an American Commander-in-Chief is to protect American lives - the first and prime responsibility charter. Is he doing it? What does he consider his first responsibility?

God bless America.

58
To Do or Not To Do

We have all heard the 'to be or not to be' phrase from Shakespeare's Hamlet:

"To be, or not to be, that is the question: Whether 'tis Nobler in the mind to suffer The Slings and Arrows of outrageous Fortune, Or to take Arms against a Sea of troubles."

The 'to be or not to be' thing stuck in my head the other day, and I couldn't get it out to make more progress on my upcoming book about the great drone attack on American life. Drones in your face will be coming soon, their targets determined and reinforced by a cashless society.

So to get rid of this annoyance, I decided to spend some time on the subject, the question: to be or not to be. I'm not sure what that quote really means, and in my quick research it seems no one is totally certain what was in Shakespeare's mind when he wrote it. So, in my extreme conservative view, I decided to analyze the quote from a strictly conservative viewpoint. This is my take on that question.

Perhaps Shakespeare asked, 'Is it better to accept that which you have, (those slings and arrows) misfortunes of having less, or should one (take up arms) make an effort, to make his or her life better? In this case referring to economic status. Perhaps Shakespeare was posing the question: 'Is it worth the extra effort to have more in life to avoid those 'slings and arrows.' In other words, 'Is it worth the effort to have or not to have?'

From my conservative viewpoint this calls forth another 'do' or 'not do.' That is: 'To do or not to do,' that is the question. Isn't 'To be or not to be' and 'To have or not to have' in the end decided by one's choice of 'To do or not to do' something for themselves?

The conservative choice and the American way is to do, not to wait for a hand out or a fair share determined by the government.

There I've done it. Now I can get back to that novel, Drones: 2025. I have 60,000 words now completed of 100,000 words planned.

God bless America.

59

Will Our Troops Fire On Patriots?

On October 15, this year, I posted a blog titled, 'Obama is Testing the Waters.' In that blog I asked the question - would our military fire on civilians if they were ordered to do so by Obama's government. This is a very, very serious question. My conclusion was yes they would. They would have no choice, because those civilians would be classified as 'terrorists' by Obama's government. I just got an email from a friend that discussed the same question. Supposedly the contents forwarded were written by a retired military general. In it he discusses this question with an active duty Army colonel. This is that forwarded email:

"Keep your uniform clean---I think we're going to need you! When I asked my colleague the Army Colonel why he thinks Obama is doing this, the reply I received from this life-long soldier and Army leader shocked me. Paraphrasing him, this is what he told me in a nut shell. He said, most branches of the service routinely engage in war games and come up with strategies and tactics on how to handle every type of military conflict and scenario that can be imagined. One of the big new battle scenarios being actively discussed in the military recently is how to handle civil unrest in the U.S. And fighting in the streets. What will the Army do if called in to fight armed civilians in the streets of the United States? How will that urban warfare be conducted? Will troops be able to fire upon other American citizens when the troops take an oath to protect American citizens?

He said many in the military are discussing the very real possibility that Obama will attempt to stay in office beyond two terms. It is being speculated that Obama will do this by declaring a state of martial law. The easiest way to declare martial law is when there is massive civil unrest and riots throughout the U.S. Thus, it is believed that Obama, and his regime, will intentionally create a situation of massive civil unrest. Some believe he has already started to implement that strategy by forcing Obamacare on everyone (when the populace did not ask for it and less than 300 people in power voted for it).

Perhaps the Obama Administration is not too concerned over the totally dysfunctional Obamacare website and the additional fact that millions will be dropped from their existing insurance policies which they already had and liked. The Obama Administration may not care if getting health care becomes more difficult and more expensive because it is all leading toward civil unrest. It is believed by some that Obamacare will only get worse and worse, and then in 2 to 3 years when people have a very difficult time getting medical treatment for themselves or their loved ones, people will get enraged.

Moreover, it is being speculated that around the same time when the frustration levels over Obamacare are hitting a critical point in 2 to 3 years, there will be a glitch in the welfare payment (or EBT) payment system. The tens of millions who rely on EBT handouts to sustain themselves will be cut off. The overwhelming majority of the EBT recipients are Black. The Obama regime will then blame the glitch on the Republicans, I.e., Republicans froze government spending which forced Obama to suspension of EBT payments. (Obama will intentionally drive spending up and up uncontrolled knowing full well that one day the Republicans will be backed into a corner and finally vote for a freeze in spending.)

Obama will create heightened racial tension by telling everyone that the White Republicans are racially motivated and did this to hurt the Black community. This manufactured racial tension, combined with growing tensions over the then-collapsing medical coverage due to Obamacare, will result in race wars and civil unrest. People will take to the streets. By the way, you should know that my colleague, the Army Colonel who is telling me all this, is Black.

He specifically commented, and outwardly expressed his embarrassment, about how Blacks have become so dependent and enslaved by the welfare system and the Democrats that it would be very easy to create civil unrest and race wars merely by cutting off, or dramatically hindering, EBT payments for only a month or so.

My colleague noted that this possibility is clearly being analyzed and discussed inside the military because such a martial law strategy is nothing new. Tyrannical and dictatorial leaders in the past have done the martial law strategy many times. He noted that dictators such as Stalin, Mussolini, and Hitler did basically the identical thing." End of quote.

My major question is: aren't we better than the Russians? If you remember, when Russian soldiers were told to fire on their civilians by Nikita Krushchev (Boris Yeltsin standing on a tank looking down the barrel of a big gun) they refused to fire on their fellow citizens. The Communists lost. In my hope of hopes, our young military people will understand and refuse to fire. It will be a hard and difficult choice. And we can't forget the possibility that many of the Islamic terrorists, now allowed to stream across our borders from the south, are real terrorists waiting for that call to arms.

My new book in progress, 'Drones: 2025,' discusses and analyzes this very important question. It should be available in January or February.

God bless America - and our military troops.

60

Our Totally Dishonest President

Barack Obama's lack of honesty is a topic that came up recently as a result of his statement, "If you like your policy, you can keep your policy," regarding the new healthcare act. Research revealed he knew that was not true when he made that claim. The only conclusion is that he intentionally lied. He knew what he said was not the truth. This was such a shock to many people - that the president would tell such a blatant lie. A little more research demonstrates that telling lies seems to be his normal nature.

Remember the Benghazi event? He immediately blamed the deaths of those four Americans killed by Islamic radicals on a totally unrelated video in Egypt. Further information revealed he knew that was a blatant untruth. This is just another example of his basic character. But, it didn't start there. Following is an even more extreme example of falsehoods by Obama. How many have forgotten his comments about his relationship with Bill Ayers? Not many know how he was connected to Ayers. Let's examine something very important about that relationship.

Obama claims he hardly knew his good friend and party pal, Bill Ayers, the man who expressed his patriotism with bombs against America. He is also the man, along with his father, who is thought to have helped launch Obama's political career. What was the ultimate purpose? Was it to support Bill Ayers' continued hate and aggression against America?

He claimed to know Ayers only as someone he casually saw in the neighborhood. He failed to reveal that he was on two boards with Bill Ayers, the Annenberg Project and the Woods Foundation, and that on at least one occasion he attended a party at Bill Ayers' home. Why did he not tell the whole and revealing truth about his association with Bill Ayers? Why did he keep that information a secret even if it were a casual acquaintance or an incidental event? What was he afraid of? If he were that non-associated with Bill Ayers why did he not say so and reveal the whole truth? What were the hidden secrets? Does not a minor deception require more questions? Obama's relationship with Ayers goes even deeper, and represents even more hidden danger to our national security.

This is an article published by Aaron Klein, January 23, 2013, that shows the insidious attack on our education system - and America, by the Islamists. Aaron Klein is WND's (WorldNetDaily) senior staff reporter and Jerusalem bureau chief. He also hosts 'Aaron Klein Investigative Radio' on New York's WABC Radio. The article begins: "A Muslim Brotherhood-linked organization has partnered with the U.S. Department of Education and the State Department to facilitate an online program aiming to connect all U.S. schools with classrooms abroad by 2016." Vartan Gregorian, a board member of the organization, the Qatar Foundation International, was appointed in 2009 to President Obama's White House Fellowships Commission. WND previously exposed that Gregorian served as a point man in granting $49.2 million in startup capital to an education-reform project founded by former Weather Underground terrorist William Ayers and chaired by Obama.

Documentation shows Gregorian was central in Ayers' recruitment of Obama to serve as the first chairman of the project, the Chicago Annenberg Challenge – a job in which Obama worked closely on a regular basis with Ayers. Obama also later said his job at the project qualified him to run for public office, as WND previously reported."

Yet, Obama claims he hardly knew Bill Ayers. This falsehood, in itself, is not necessarily important. The important point is that the president of the United States, Barack Obama, is not honor bound to be guided by truth. He has demonstrated too many times that his words cannot be trusted. How can a leader lead if he or she is not guided, at least to some degree, by honesty? America cannot be at its best and highest if its leader is not at least partially honest, and demonstrates the best interest of the United States as his guiding principle.

Do we have any reason to believe him when he says, "God bless America?" Should we believe anything he says, especially about his plans and intentions for the future of the United States? My latest book, 'King Obama: America's Greatest Danger,' explains many more of his plans and deceptions.

God bless America.

61

Moving Along

If I can ever get off these darn blogs, I might get my new novel finished. I had good progress the last two days. I wrote a larger blog and also got 3000 words further on the novel. Now up to 53,000 words of the planned 1000T word novel. Still not sure of the title; maybe 'Dark Drones' or 'Drones 2025.' Maybe even 'Devil Drones.' Anyway, now I can see the end moving forward. I don't outline before I begin and let the story find its own way.

I guess I've been influenced somewhat by two sources. One is '1984' by George Orwell which describes a tightly controlled authoritarian society. The other is the movie 'Soylent Green' which is based on a book by Harry Harrison titled, 'Make Room! Make Room!' Anyone who saw that movie knows what the 'Make Room' refers to. So far, my new novel is finding its way to situations described by those two references.

These darn blogs!

62

Our Declining Society

I heard a question this morning on a news program that not only caught my attention, but it should also be a question that concerns every American. That question was: 'Is America a declining society?' The question went further and considered the factor of 'trust' among ourselves. The moderator suggested a poll revealed we don't trust each other as much as we did before. Although I'm still trying to concentrate on finishing my novel, I had to stop and make a comment about that question.

I don't agree with the conclusion of that poll or that finding about trust among citizens. My personal contacts and the people I deal with in person and on the phone all seem honest and as eager to be a positive part of society as I am. Some people might be forgetful or not follow through on a promise, but I think that might be a symptom of just being lazy rather than being dishonest. In the last two years, I've witnessed only two blatant cases or real dishonesty. One was an eBay transaction where a seller refused to send an item I had paid for. But, in that case he got kicked off eBay - which suggests we have systems guided by honesty. The other case of blatant dishonesty is the current one perpetuated by Barack Obama and his false statements about the health care law - period! But, I think that reflects more an example of his personal character than that of society in general. Society should not be judged by the actions or character of one individual.

Perhaps, however, we are allowing ourselves to accept the basics of a 'declining' society. Two conditions present themselves as clear examples. First, is our acceptance and acquiescence of declining quality of produced goods and services. The other is lack of a sincere and effective effort to educate our children.

An example of declining quality is clothing. In the old days, when you bought pants, size 34X30, they were 34 inches around and 30 inches in measured length. Now, they could be 33 or 35 in the waist, and 29 to 33 in length. Worse yet, the bright color fades after the second wash. Even worse yet, the front pockets are so short you can hardly get one finger in your pockets. Many have waist bands so low they don't reach the waist. It makes a guy say "yikes." Yes, we are declining in our expectations of quality - a level of quality that Americans were proud to produce. Our clothing is made out of country where internal domestic pride of quality does not guide the finished product, and we are accepting it.

Our worst decline is in education effectiveness. It is in proven decline. Education effectiveness should be our greatest asset and one that we should be most proud of. It can never be great again until the federal government removes itself from that process. Other than supreme arrogance the problem with government intervention with education is that they try to control, manipulate and test. They will continue to destroy education effectiveness until they learn that student motivation, to want to do it themselves for what they perceive as a reasonable goal, is the most important tool. I have two books on the market, now, that describe how to reach that process. In short, government must not dictate, they must encourage personal goals then facilitate. (Added: Perhaps Obama's current administration is not only allowing educate to erode, but is trying to accelerate that process. A less-educated society is a society easier to totally control.)

God bless America.

63

Constitution "Gets In the Way"

As I've suggested many times at this blog site and in my books, Obama will not give up the presidency at the end of his current term. According to the 22nd Amendment to our Constitution, two terms or ten years total is the maximum one may serve as president of the United States. He already said, "The Constitution gets in the way of many things I would like to do." To me, this suggests he has no respect for the intention and purpose for our Constitution. Can one who has no respect for a foundation be trusted to comply with that foundation?

I would like to expound further on this topic, but I'm still trying to finish my new novel about the coming influence of drones. Tentatively the title is, 'Drones 2025.' I finally reached the halfway mark, 50,000 words, but still have that many to go. Maybe I'll have it finished in February - if I don't spend too much time writing blogs.

Anyway, here are two references that show beginnings of Obama's plan to remain in office - perhaps forever or until he moves on to bigger and better things. One is a professor who says he should be allowed to be re-elected. The other shows how the 'Organizing for Action' group is becoming more involved. Tie the two together and what do you have?

http://politix.topix.com/homepage/9176-obama-needs-a-third-term-says-op-ed-in-major-newspaper

http://swampland.time.com/2013/11/11/obamas-grassroots-moneybags-the-top-19-organizing-for-action-donors/

Enough of that. Now it's time to get back to the drones.

God bless America.

64

Lying Lips

Yesterday, I was scanning through my recent book, King Obama: America's Greatest Danger, when I read across one of my Bible quotes. That quote is:

"Lying lips are an abomination to the Lord, but those who act faithfully are His delight." Proverbs12:22.

While I read perhaps another paragraph, my subconscious wouldn't abandon that comment. Finally I realized why, so I went back and read the quote again. Then I made the important connection. That quote wasn't regarding a spontaneous single lie spoken without forethought. It was regarding 'lying lips.' It was referring to one who lies for a purposeful reason. It's the description of a 'deceiver,' one who deceives.

Of course there are many who lie. Some are 'little white lies' and some are to protect one's image or to discredit another's. Some other more serious lies concern legal matters that have graver consequences. But, who among us at this time of our history, has lips that lie so greatly his lies could change the course of history for our nation - period? Here, I will not say or write the man's name, other than in the book title, above. However, I believe he has now earned a biblical name of 'the deceiver.'

The Bible introduces the deceiver in the Garden of Eden. He's the one who convinced Eve to taste the forbidden fruit in the garden, because it would give her insight and knowledge. He also said she should not believe what God told her. He, that 'Old Serpent,' said God is merely an illusion. She followed the deceiver's persuasion and broke the covenant. The Garden of Eden was lost forever. That deceiver continued to cast his lies throughout history, and exists just as powerfully today.

Following that deceiver's example, our new deceiver continues to discredit the Lord, and he continues to deceive his fellow man for his own purposes. There are many examples of his blasphemy, which I have repeated often at this blog site, including: "We are no longer a Christian nation," "turn to their Bibles and guns," and covering the symbol of Jesus while making a speech at a university.

One of his lies was so great that he was finally forced to admit it was a deception. But he included qualifiers to that admission. He can't get totally away from deceiving. His lie about the health care act is so great that it could change the prosperity and morality of our nation. It's designed for wealth redistribution, to make everyone equally poor, and to make everyone support killing babies in the womb.

But, should we expect anything more honest from this man of deception? After all, he wears his predecessor's icon on the ring he so proudly exhibits. Two serpents lie coiled on his ring - the one he removed only to be used for his wedding ring. Will America be cast out of her 'Garden of Eden' for following this great deceiver?

God bless and protect America.

65

A Little Side Trip

Ever wonder how a story about a turtle who thought he was a rabbit might end? I didn't either until I decided to write that scene as part of a larger story that included many other strange, and almost true if you use your wildest imagination, scenes. Other unusual almost true scenes include Old Mother Hubbard's dog named Boney. Mother Hubbard told Boney to go find his own bones. In his search to find bones, Boney encountered many other almost true, imaginary characters. These include the shoe house, where there were so many children nobody knew what to do; Little Miss Muffet's spider, named Creepy, who just wanted to make friends; and, Hickory, Dickory, and Dock, who like to run up and down clocks. And, of course, we could never forget the witch who likes to bake Hansel and Gretel cookies.

Holiday season is upon us. If you would like a free PDF download of this really timely and earth-moving, important and almost true, story for your kids, grand-kids, or great grand- kids coming to visit during Thanksgiving or Christmas, just click on the link below and your free PDF version will be downloaded instantly. You may pass it on and share it as many times as you would like. Happy Thanksgiving, and happy holidays. The title is: Wishing Wells and Broken Tales.

www.authorsden.com/adstorage/1496/WW-Words-AD-Free.pdf

God bless America.

66

Orders to Fire

Recently, I wrote a blog that asked the question: would the U.S. military fire upon citizens if the president ordered them to do so. In this scenario, I asked the question what if Barack Obama decided that American citizens who were defending themselves should be classified as 'terrorists.' This question is connected to the idea that Obama will not give up the presidency at the end of his current term. Would he declare 'martial law' if he deemed it necessary to prevent a growing terrorist threat thereby justifying that action.

I just learned that a precedent has already be set, many years ago, in 1932. This is a link that describes that action against American citizens. Although it's not exactly for the same reason, it nevertheless demonstrates that a president will order military action against American citizens. Will Obama use it for another purpose?

http://www.youtube.com/watch_popup?feature=player_embedd
ed&v=sNOsIB5VMSQ

67

Why So Much Ammunition?

I've mentioned this before, but I think it's worthy of a reminder many more times before the end of Obama's administration - if there will be an end to Obama's administration. This reminder is regarding the purchase of 1.6 billion rounds of ammunition by the Obama administration. That's not a typo - it's real - BILLION. Why? According to those who have current knowledge that's equivalent to enough ammunition to fight the war in Afghanistan for seven more years - yes, SEVEN years.

When questioned, the answer given was 'for training purposes.' But, why would anyone use half a million rounds of hollow-point ammunition for training? Hollow-point bullets are used only when deadly force is intended - never ever for training. They are more expensive - and they shatter on impact.

Recently I read an article that suggested the Obama administration was trying a back-door approach to gun control. Consuming all the available ammunition on the market, and planned to be on the market, would, in effect, create the same result as strict gun control. What good is a gun without bullets? Obama's actions to control guns create two important questions. Why is he afraid for American citizens to be armed? What might happen if ammunition is not available on the regular market for American citizens?

Why is Obama afraid for American citizens to be armed?

Would Obama be afraid for American citizens to be armed if he didn't have something in mind that would cause American citizens to be concerned about his plans or his actions for or against America? What makes him think citizens would feel a need to be armed? Is it for the reason our Founding Fathers, in the Constitution, allowed citizens to arm themselves. That purpose was to oppose tyranny and despotism.

What might happen if Obama keeps citizens from getting ammunition?

In my discussions with sporting and gun stores, I was told that Russia would fill the void if ammunition was not available. Supposedly, gun store dealers feel Russia would keep the market flowing - regardless how much the Obama administration bought off the market. On the other hand how serious could that get. If Obama banned Russian imports of ammunition, would it then be sold underground like drugs? Could that become a very serious event between two countries that already don't trust each other?

Want to read more, and many more interesting ideas about gun control and gun prohibition in the United States? Check out my two novels: America 20XX: The New World Order, and 666: Mark of the Beast. You might be surprised how often fiction is not always fiction.

God bless America.

68

Human Foundations

My fear of the plans from a certain leader among us grows deeper each day. Possibly the culture, principles, and aims of that leader is the foundation of the one destined to challenge all that's good within humanity. Most of us have been trained to accept or have instinctively adopted the humanities of loving our neighbors, sharing our rewards, respecting the goals of others, and in general terms, respecting ourselves and loving our neighbors.

I believe there is a leader among us who is destined to turn these ideals upside down. One is mentioned many times in the Bible as the deceiver and the lawless one. I went to google and searched 'the deceiver.' The following information was one of the results of that inquiry. Of course, it's from the Bible.

Proverbs 6: 16-19 says there are six things that the Lord hates, seven that are an abomination to him: A proud look, a lying tongue, and hands that shed innocent blood, a heart that devises wicked plans, feet that be swift in running to mischief, a false witness who speaketh lies, and one who sows discord among brethren.

After thinking about this information from the Bible, my trust in this 'great world leader' continues to wane more and more. Automatically, several questions popped into my head:

1 What leader among us carries a proud look - often by turning his head into a 'superiority' cocked position?

2. What leader among us has a lying tongue? One of his lies about the healthcare act was so great and profound that he recently had to finally admit it was a lie. There are many more we know of that he hasn't admitted yet; consider his comment about the cause of the Benghazi slaughter. He said it was caused by a 'video.' Was that a lie or was that the truth?

3. What leader among us allowed innocent blood to be shed by refusing to send help to those innocents slaughtered in Benghazi? Why did he send them there to that danger in the first place? Why were members of Seal Team Six ambushed and slaughtered after he announced Seal Team Six had killed their great Islamic hero, Osama Bin Laden?

4. What are his plans? Are they to encourage positive principles guided by humanity and Christianity, or are they to force compliance to the dictates of that other 'unknown' god? Why does he not follow our Constitution, and make his own laws simply by dictate? Why is he encouraging people to perform acts that are identified as an 'abomination' in the Bible?

5. What leader among us actively encourages discord among brothers? He plays the rich against the poor, the Republicans against the Democrats, citizens against non-citizens, and the educated against the uneducated. He clearly and purposefully sows

discord - for his selfish gain of more power.

Will his power plans mature far enough to fulfill Bible prophesy? At this time, who can stop him? Perhaps there is still time, and a way to stop him. Don't forget - today is Sunday. Have a blessed day!

God bless America.

69

Once Upon A Time

Once upon a time. I don't know why, but I've been drawn to two new programs on television. They are: Once Upon A Time, and Once Upon A Time in Wonderland. I can't keep the storylines apart in these two programs - if there are any storylines at all. They seem a mixed hodge-podge of Snow White, the little Mermaid, the seven dwarfs, Captain Hook, the evil queen, Wendy, Rumpelstiltskin and Peter Pan, plus many others. (That little mermaid is really cute. Maybe that's why I continue to watch the program.) Peter Pan is the 'bad guy' in these plots, if they are plots, and if there is a bad guy. Anyway Peter Pan is trying to play the bad guy part, keeping all his subjects at bay. It's a total distortion of 'once upon a time' when we thought fairy tales were positive - and fun.

This great turnaround reminds me of another once - once upon a time. I remember, once upon at time, when I was very young, 6 or 7, when every American was a real and true American. I remember when the 'soldiers' came home from the war and America was a happy, proud, and exuberant place filled with positive ambitions and great expectations of the future. No one stood on the sidelines waiting for that free handout from the government. They were the government!

The three great themes at that time were: Jobs, Education, and God. Many returning warriors had learned their abilities during the war, and entered schools and job-training programs in great numbers to do something for themselves - and to continue the great success and leadership position of this great nation. This was 'once upon a time' when we had our clear example of the 'Greatest Generation' leading a great nation. That was 'once upon a time.' How have we changed so drastically?

Now we have a president who openly hates what America stands for, and is trying to change its total character to match that of the rest of the world. To him, we have been 'too arrogant.' He stated he wants to reduce our standing in the world so the Islamists will not think we believe we are 'above' them. He never suggests a proactive and independent role for individual citizens - only to become dependent citizens. He appoints only people who despise the success of America to influential positions. His themes from his verbose mouth are completely opposite from: Jobs, Education, and God. How can a nation be led to further greatness when its leader voices only contempt and disdain for its great success?

Once upon a time we had those things, those ideals. What

happened? Is it Peter Pan or the Pied Piper leading us into cultural and economic deterioration?

God bless America.

70

Excerpt from Fiction or Coming Events

My new novel is still progressing well - I think. I just completed 39,000 words of the planned 100,000 words. I'm still not sure of the title, but now plan for it to be one of several: Dark Drones, Fire From the Sky, Death Drones, or perhaps even, The Antichrist Drones. I'll wait until it's finished to decide the exact title. I have no clue how it will end, since I don't outline before I begin writing. Anyway, this is an excerpt I just finished to top off 39,000 words. It's about a character named Bill who was chased by a group of 'Others' and is hiding in a wooded area. It's his first encounter with a drone - he didn't see:

"He pushed through the brush to the other side then stood at the edge of that road, looking across, wondering how long it would take and what experiences he would encounter crossing that twenty short yards. Was that a bird crossing the outer edge of the moon; but what bird coasts at that altitude during the night? He discounted what he thought he had seen then peeked up and down the road. Nothing was moving; perhaps this was his best opportunity to get to the other side; another chance for freedom.

Instead of running as he had planned, his instincts forced him to creep when his shoes touched the pavement. Perhaps running would bring too much noise and movement that could more easily be heard and seen. Moving lower and slower perhaps would attract less attention to anyone not intently focused on that road. He paused halfway when his peripheral vision saw that bird again as it moved across the moon's glow. A strange thought blinked as he looked at the bird; the bird never moved its wings.

Bill didn't really know what had happened as he lay supine on the black asphalt. He had seen the bird's sudden spark and felt a strong tingle in his whole body. Then, suddenly it was a shock that slammed his body to the road. For a moment he smelled fire and fumes of burning flesh, then nothing. He was just there; eyes seeing only the bright moon outlining what appeared as that bird. How big was it? He couldn't tell. Was it near or far? He didn't know. The moon dimmed and he saw nothing. He didn't see or feel anything when the Others' knife man arrived and unsheathed his blade."

I had planned to finish this book in December, but now it seems it might be in late January. If I play more golf than I planned, it might be February. Maybe cold weather will determine how soon it gets finished.

God bless America.

71

True Colors

Barack Obama's true colors are finally exposing themselves. He has been a great deceiver; some consider a liar, for the sole purpose of having his way and gaining more power. There are many deceptions from Obama, but the first two that come to mind are: "If you like your health care plan you can keep it," and the Benghazi slaughter was caused by a, "video."

He exhibits many other deceptions to the degree that nothing he says can really be considered as honest, truthful - and honorable. As Americans, we should expect our leader, our president, to be guided by at least a minimal level of what most people consider, 'honor.' Honor, honesty, and truth are not his guiding light. What guides him to represent an honor level lower than even those weaker in character in our society? Perhaps his basic character - and his ambition of his destiny.

But, that should not be a surprise. His most prized possession, his ring, is a personal representation of his deceptive arrogance. Perhaps it's also a representation of his assignment - that destiny planned for him ages ago. And, he proudly wears a representation of that destiny - his ring.

Displayed on his ring are two coiled serpents. Many verses in the Bible refer to Satan as a serpent; starting in the Garden of Eden in Genesis, and moving to the church at Pergamos, in Revelation. The Bible also refers many times to the serpent as a deceiver - one who doesn't tell the truth, and speaks falsehoods to gain the confidence and support of his gullible followers. That has been the exact description of Barack Obama. It seems he speaks the truth only when it benefits him, personally, in some way.

My book, Obama's Ring: The Seat of Satan, connects the danger represented in that ring he wears to the danger America faces today due to many of his actions, and connections with the Muslim Brotherhood. For the past three months, this book has also been my best seller. Apparently, more people are beginning to question Obama's character - and his intentions for our great nation. What's the best part of this book? It gives many correlations between what the Bible says will happen - and what Barack Obama is doing to us. Be aware.

God bless America.

72

We Must Be Guided By Government

In my previous blog I expressed a little ray of hope that America could escape the despotic aims of Obama, his administration, and his shadow government made up of socialists and Islamists. But now I've reverted back to my original thoughts that the man has no limits to his zeal for total power and total control of America - and who knows where else. Obama was caught in a clear, bold, and blatant lie. But, what does he do? Does he repent; does he apologize? Absolutely not!

When he proclaimed, "If you like your plan and your doctor, you can keep your plan and your doctor - PERIOD!" he knew he was lying. According to reports, some in his administration had advised him that was not truthful when he planned that speech - repeated many times. He knew it was a lie, yet he continued to repeat it. Now that his brazen lie has been made public, what is his reaction?

His reaction is to call American citizens too stupid to think for themselves. He now says that what should be clear to us simpletons is that if you like your health care plan - and it's a plan that fits into what the administration considers a good plan - then you can keep your health care plan. That means the government - particularly Barack Obama - knows what's best for us. It means we can't think for ourselves. It means if we are that stupid, then we must be protected from ourselves by a totalitarian government. That means Barack Hussein Obama must remain in total power to provide that protection.

If his lies are that bold and blatant, what can we expect from the man in the future? What beholds us during the last year of his current term - not necessarily his 'last' term?

God bless America.

73

Maybe There's Still Hope

Maybe there's still hope for America to remain a great country. Since Barack Obama was elected president of the United States, I've seen nothing but long-term despair for our great nation. I thought I saw, on the horizon, a great despotic takeover by one whose ambition was greater than the future of one nation. In my view, every action he has accomplished or tried to accomplish has been contrary to positive leadership and the sound principles of a free market system that guided America to its greatness. Now, maybe - just maybe, a new tide has turned that will block Obama's personal despotic agenda to lead the United States to third-world status, or below.

What's this positive sign? Presently, it's reported that Obama's approval rating is now down to 42 percent. Of course that could be reversed, but for the moment that's new bright sunshine to enlighten a new day, a bright new day for our country. This is not to say Barack Obama has changed his mind or his agenda. Instead, it's to suggest that maybe more people have come to see his true colors - and they are not red, white, and blue. Perhaps the despair growing from the results of his Obamacare plan is showing more of his doles that free stuff is not always free. Often 'free' means there's a greater price to be paid at the end of the game.

Are more people in the United States getting smarter - or have they only been in hiding waiting for more information to make a decision. I'm much more optimistic about the future of our great nation today than I've been in over four years.

This story is quite similar to the outline in my book, America 20XX: The New World Order. In this novel, America almost loses its freedom, but at the last moment something happens to return freedom from the brink of disaster. It's a detailed lesson regarding the implications of gun control laws

God bless America.

74

On Being Patriotic

Watching Obama's actions and listening to his words the past few years have created a great question for me, and I'm sure for many other people as well. As a retired military officer who gave my best during my years of service, including service in Vietnam, I consider myself very patriotic to a country that has given me so many opportunities to serve and to succeed. And, I'm positive many other people, veterans or not, have felt just as proud of America and as patriotic as I have.

And, although many of us have gone through stages where we didn't agree with the president at that time, we nevertheless served and did our regular jobs with pride that our nation was the example for the world, and our leaders were performing to keep that status for America. Although I disagreed with Lyndon Johnson's war policies regarding Vietnam while I was there, and his social policies to make more American citizens more dependent on the government, I still felt his heart and his efforts were in trying to do the best he could to sustain our great nation. He just didn't have the right answers. But - at that time, who really did? Our national policies were to defeat Communism by stopping the domino effect. What most didn't know is that there were not that many dominoes to sustain Communism. At least Johnson acted in what he perceived as the best policies for the good of

Democracy and America.

My perception of Barack Obama, however, is different. My question is: how can I support and trust our president if I truly believe his only purpose and goal is to destroy our great nation? How can I be more patriotic? How can I support his policies? How can I wish him great success? If I felt, in any way, his motives were positive for America I would be his greatest supporter. And, without giving a president our full support, how can we feel we are still patriotic? How can we wish him great success in his efforts? These questions create a great dilemma. If we support our president, and his goals are to destroy our nation, can we consider ourselves proud patriots? On the other hand, if we don't support the president and his policies are we less patriotic?

I want to be a positive patriot, but Obama's actions and words do not allow me that freedom. He has proven to be untrustworthy by all his untruths and deceptions - and there are many.

God bless America.

75

Obama's 'Bump In the Road'

How have we allowed the question about the slaughter of four brave Americans to change from its original stance? If you remember, the questions about Benghazi were: 1. Where was Hillary Clinton and why didn't she respond to requests for more security and protection for the ambassador and his subordinates? 2. Where was Barack Obama while those attacks were happening and why didn't he initiate some action to at least give the impression that he cared about their safety? Obviously, he gave a stand-down order then went to bed to rest comfortably while four brave citizens were being slaughtered and tortured. Soon afterward, he called it a 'bump in the road' not what it really was - an act of terror by his non-terrorist Islamists.

Hillary Clinton's whereabouts are still a secret mystery; she has never said where she was or what she was doing. Obama took one phone call from the secretary of defense and the chairman of the Joint Chiefs of Staff, and then he disappeared never to be heard from again - until his fund-raising trip the next day in Las Vegas. Those important questions are fading into never-land as time passes.

Those critical questions no longer exist. Now the new question is: when will those terrorists be caught and justice fulfilled? Obama's Alinsky tactics are working again. Wait long enough - then plant a distraction away from the most important situation.

It seems that to Obama and Hillary the brutal murder of four proud Americans was only a 'bump in the road' that 'made no difference.' If an ambassador representing a great country such as ours is considered only a bump in the road and not worthy of protection, I wonder how much Obama would be concerned about protecting my life - or yours - or yours. What is the primary purpose for a commander-in-chief, anyway? Is it to ignore major responsibilities and go to fund-raisers?

God bless America.

76

Waiting for Hillary

I just heard Hillary Clinton's first political speech for her campaign for president in 2016. Although she was speaking for the Democratic governor candidate in Virginia, her comments were clearly for herself. When her real campaign begins, I plan to submit a daily blog. It will be: "Where was Hillary when four brave Americans were slaughtered in Benghazi?" She was the one most directly responsible for their lives and their safety, yet she never said where she was. Was she sleeping or just not interested enough to watch it on television?

Also, her comment regarding the event, "What difference does it make?" must never be forgotten by any citizen who loves and respects our great nation - and those who put their lives in danger to protect it. But, according to her glib comment: "What difference does it make," I only hope her opponents in either the primary or general election have enough guts to make these comments a constant 'In your face' issue. We must press the demand that anyone in authority in our government must place a priority on protecting American citizens. That's our federal government's first priority and first responsibility.

Obama and Hillary treated the slaughter of four brave American citizens as just another event of the day. Neither has ever said where they were or what they were doing, except Obama. He took time to give the 'stand-down' order not to save those brave Americans.

I hope when her campaign begins, millions of American patriots raise the theme, every day: "Where was Hillary" and "What difference does it make?" It must never be swept under the dirty political rug and forgotten.

God bless America.

77

Another Obama Connection

How is Barack Obama associated with and supporting the Muslim Brotherhood? An article written by Raven Clabough of by The New American, Tuesday, 24 September 2013, titled: 'Muslim Brotherhood Linked to Malik Obama and Obama Administration,' gives a clue. This is part of that article:

"President Obama's half-brother, Malik Obama may be added to Egypt's terror watch list as a result of his alleged ties to the Muslim Brotherhood. Malik also serves as the executive secretary of the Dawa Organization, a group created by the government of Sudan, considered by the United States State Department to be a terrorist state. According to WND, Malik also served as the best man at Barack Obama's wedding to Michelle in 1992.

Malik is currently being investigated by the Egyptian government for possible terrorist connections because of his role in the Islamic Dawa Organization (IDO), as well as IDO's umbrella organization, the Muslim Brotherhood. The IDO's mission is to spread Wahhabist Islam across Africa.

According to a news report from an Egyptian media source, provided by former PLO member Walid Shoebat, a complaint has been filed with the Egyptian Attorney General against Malik Obama: The complaint requests that Malik Obama, a resident of the United States, be summoned for questioning regarding his terrorist ties, and seeks permission to declare Malik a defendant outside Egypt diplomatically, through the Ministry of Foreign Affairs. Malik has also been identified as an attendee at an IDO conference in Khartoum, the capital of Sudan, which was also attended by Sudanese President Omar Al-Bashir, a man wanted by the International Criminal Court for crimes against humanity. Bashir's regime gave Christians until March 1, 2012 to leave North Sudan, but many were stranded, leaving them as open targets for Muslims. Foreign missionaries have been deported under Bashir and churches have been bulldozed.

The complaint also references Tahani al-Gebali, former chancellor and current advisor to the Constitutional Court of Egypt, who levied accusations that Malik was linked to the Muslim Brotherhood. Gebali said that Malik was "one of the architects" of the investments made by the Muslim Brotherhood in Egypt. Gebali had also threatened to expose the Obama administration's support for the Muslim Brotherhood in Egypt. Gebali contends that the

Obama administration supported the Morsi government even after Morsi welcomed the Muslim Brotherhood into the government. "The Obama administration cannot stop us," Gebali said, as reported by Egyptian television. "We need to open the files and begin court sessions. The Obama administration knows that they supported terrorism. We will open the files and begin court sessions."

Egyptian prosecutors are expected to produce evidence that reveals the Obama administration's support of the Muslim Brotherhood. WND writes, "Egyptian government prosecutors plan to introduce evidence Muslim Brotherhood leaders in Cairo received bribes paid in amounts as large as $850,000 a year each from the Obama administration in Washington via the U.S. Embassy in Cairo."

Last year, WND reported that the Barack H. Obama Foundation, which is owned and run by Malik, received a very unusual retroactive tax-exempt approval determination letter from the IRS, signed by former head of the IRS tax-exempt division Lois Lerner. That approval came at the same time that the IRS had been persecuting conservative and religious organizations that had applied for tax-exempt status. Prior to the letter of approval, the foundation had been illegally operating as a tax exempt organization without actually receiving tax exempt status.

Further, WND reported in October that the Mama Sarah Obama Foundation, created on behalf of Obama's step-grandmother in Kenya, transferred funds raised from U.S. corporations and individuals to send Kenyan students to radical Wahhabist madrassas in Saudi Arabia. According to BW Central, there is no evidence that the funds built homes in any part of Kenya for orphans and HIV/AIDS victims (the supposed purpose of the foundation), but there is evidence that the funds were being used to fund the Recreation and Rest Center in Kenya, where Malik's 12 wives live, a facility that includes a restaurant and a mosque.

Links between the Obama administration and the Muslim Brotherhood may not come as a complete surprise. InvestigativeProject.org reports, "Six American Islamist activists who work with the Obama administration are Muslim Brotherhood operatives who enjoy strong influence over U.S. policy." Front Page Magazine identified the six operatives:

Arif Alikhan — assistant secretary for policy development for the U.S. Department of Homeland Security.

Mohammed Elibiary — homeland security advisor.

Rashad Hussain — special envoy to the Organization of the Islamic Conference (OIC).

Salam al-Marayati — Obama advisor, founder of Muslim Public Affairs Council and its current executive director.

Imam Mohamed Magid — Obama's sharia czar, Islamic Society of North America.

Eboo Patel — advisory council on Faith-Based Neighborhood Partnerships.

(An analysis of these six is also detailed in my current book, King Obama: America's Greatest Danger.)

Meanwhile, Obama has not given any indication that he opposes the work of his half-brother.

And, what of Obama's support of the Muslim Brotherhood members and supporters who are in his administration. He just gave a big promotion to one of his favorites, as reported by WND.com by Chelsea Schilling 9-16-2013:

The Obama administration has promoted a Homeland Security adviser – who is a self-declared Egyptian Muslim Brotherhood supporter – to senior fellow within the Cabinet-level department of the federal government.

Mohamed Elibiary, who was appointed to the Department of Homeland Security Advisory Council by former Secretary Janet Napolitano in 2010, tweeted Sept. 12 that he has been reappointed to the position and promoted.

Just one year after he was first appointed to the council, PJ Media reported, "Elibiary may have been given access to a sensitive database of state and local intelligence reports, and then allegedly shopped some of those materials to a media outlet. He allegedly used the documents to claim the [Texas Department of Public safety] was promoting 'Islamophobia.'"

According to the report, a "left-leaning media outlet" confirmed that Elibiary had provided "reports marked FOUO [For Official Use Only]," claiming it was proof of Texas Gov. Rick Perry's "Islamophobia."

PJ Media added, Texas DPS Director Steve McCraw "confirmed that Elibiary has access to the Homeland Security State and Local Intelligence Community of Interest (HS SLIC) database, which contains hundreds of thousands of intelligence reports and products that are intended for intelligence sharing between law enforcement agencies."

Just wondering: Is Barack Obama allowed to have secret and unrecorded meetings with anyone? Does he ever have those meetings? Who is Barack Obama?

God bless America.

78

Forced To Survival

My upcoming book, 'Dark Drones (or Death Drones, or Blood Drone),' is still progressing well. I'm now up to 30T words of 100T. I was really putting fingers to keyboard until yesterday. A friend called and wanted to go fishing. Who in their right mind would want to go fishing in South Mississippi? Anyway, I humored him. We went fishing on the Pearl River bordering MS and LA, a few miles from New Orleans. We caught 25 to 30 largemouth bass each, throwing most of them back. I kept 8, which I had to clean - glad I didn't keep more.

Anyway, this is an excerpt from my last writing before I went fishing. In it, Richard and Marlene had just escaped from the Others, who intended to kill them, and were on their way to join Marty and Janice, who were already at the survival site. In the story, I intend to explore many primitive survival ideas, including survival food, which I learned as a youth growing up in the hill country in central Mississippi. This semi survival guide is designed for a real-life, current-day purpose - just in case our current presidential administration goes too far. Excerpt:

"Richard remembered most of the trails leading toward the survival camp, but many more intersecting paths had developed since his last visit. There hadn't been any hunting the past few years, since weapons had been banned for ordinary citizens, so Richard figured more deer, raccoons, and wild boar had been roaming freely, and growing in larger numbers. Perhaps that was a good thing for their survival, he imagined, if this despotic situation continued for who knows how long. They preferred to move slowly along the trail, anyway, so Marty and Janice would have time to be awake and alert when they arrived. The last thing they wanted was to startle them; they would certainly be apprehensive about any noise.

During the first ten minutes, the flora and scenes changed several times along the trail. Marlene didn't notice the different vegetation at first, until she had eaten most of her blackberries. When they paused at an intersecting trail, she pointed and asked, "What's that stringy short bush with the little round berries; they look dark blue, about the size of a pea?"

Richard glanced up from trying to determine which path to take and said it was a huckleberry bush, like a wild blueberry. "They're edible, very tasty, if you can get them before the birds and squirrels do."

"And, so many squirrels this morning," she replied. "Why are there so many?"

"The d--- government confiscated everybody's guns, except those we hid away long ago. Thank God, some of us saw this coming; too many others thought banning guns was the right thing to do - for our safety." He pointed to the left trail and said, "This is the way; it's heading more eastward, toward the sun." Then he grumbled, "Nothing the government has ever done is for our benefit and safety; it always penalizes somebody and takes away somebody's freedom. They're nothing more than legalized terrorists."

"And, when they want to hide their atrocities, they send in their murderous cohorts, the Others." She followed Richard along the chosen trail then added, "Their supporters accept what they do and any actions they take in the name of security."

"Those d--- Doles," Richard replied. "As long as the government keeps giving them free stuff, and promises of more free stuff; they'll support everything the d--- government does; even beheading people who try to do what's right."

"Maybe they're just afraid not to support the government, Richard. Maybe they feel they have no choice."

"Maybe not now, but at one time they did have a choice. Then their lazy greed blinded their common sense of being patriotic and productive citizens. Their greed and laziness destroyed everything."

They walked ten more paces before Marlene said, "Well, we can't take it all back, now; we'll have to survive the best we can until something changes; until someone strong enough to change things takes over."

"It might be a long time. They're in control of everything now, except folks like us. I don't know how long we can stay free." End of excerpt.

After fishing yesterday morning, I couldn't concentrate enough to type yesterday evening, so I decided to wait until today. Then this morning, I had to go try to improve my golf game. Tomorrow, I have to attend a family reunion a hundred miles away. Okay - maybe I can finish the book in January instead of December.

God bless America.

79

Our Last President

Are there any doubters who really believe Obama will not remain president for another term - or endless terms? Originally, my thought about this was based on the probability that he would declare some type of terrorist or security emergency toward the end of his current term, then declare 'martial law' to control the emergency - without the emergency ever ending to return to normalcy. And, in my thoughts, that's still likely to happen.

Obama is already beginning to purge the military to do this - to fill the military with supporters for his agenda. The chairman of the Joint Chiefs of Staff, General Martin Dempsey, is a lackey that will support him whatever he does. Just last week, two general officers in charge of nuclear weapons were fired. How many more will be fired or retired during the next two years? Who will be taking their places?

Recently, however, I've acknowledged there is an easier and equal possibility for Obama to achieve his goal of never leaving office. He is too power-driven, or filled with more sinister ambitions, to go away quietly.

How easy it would be for Obama to declare himself eligible for another term, or endless terms, with just two more appointments to the Supreme Court and having Eric Holder to challenge the Constitution. The Twenty-second Amendment could be overturned without amending the Constitution. Eric Holder and an Obama Supreme Court could simply nullify that Amendment. Yes, right or wrong, they have the guts and the disdain of our Constitution to do that! Do you think he has more character and patriotism than to do something like this? Just look at how he's treating World War II heroes. The man doesn't even know the definition of character, honor, or patriotism.

Obama will accomplish it some way. He and his Islamic radical Muslim Brotherhood cohorts will not let this opportunity pass. And, what about a 'shadow government' already in place to give Obama greater powers when that happens? Who is likely the leader of this 'shadow government?' Obama has already bowed to him at the beginning of his first administration. Who else could it be?

My next blog will explain how his 'Doles' will support his activities.

God bless America.

80

The Personal Choice

This is a letter to the editor that appeared today in the Biloxi Sun Herald, our local newspaper on the Mississippi Gulf Coast:

"I have read Letters to the Editor about the impossibility and the foolishness of thinking an armed citizenry can successfully take on the U.S. military if the country is unresponsive to its citizens.

The American colonists took on the most powerful, sophisticated military in the world and won. The Vietnamese took on the French and defeated them in 1954 and then fought us, the most powerful military in the world, to a standstill. The Afghan rebels took on the USSR and drove the Soviets out, and are so far undefeated against the U.S. and our allies after a decade of fighting. We see rebels taking on a powerful Syrian military and at least holding their own if not winning.

History tells us time after time that an armed citizenry can take on much stronger military force and frequently win. Additionally, if such a revolution took place in the U.S. today, much of the military would refuse to fight their brothers if they felt their cause was just."

Why do I consider this letter important enough to post it here on Authorsden? I wrote a blog similar to this awhile back posing almost the same question: what would our military people do in case there is a conflict between our despotic administration and our country? The author of this letter seems to believe that our military would not fire on American citizens, and would do what the Russians did when Boris Yeltsin stood in front of the government's Russian tanks. They turned and supported Yeltsin - creating a new form of government in Russia.

In case of a domestic uprising, I'm not sure what might happen. It's possible that the author of that 'letter to the editor' might be wrong. We have current examples of government forces firing on civilians without proven just cause. The two most current examples are David Koresh and the Branch Dividians, and Ruby Ridge. In these examples, there were no clear reasons for attack, yet approximately 30 innocent people were killed by police forces. The only allegations were that they 'were doing something wrong.'

What if Obama, in his continuing war on American culture, traditions, and our Constitution, designated a 'radical' group of citizens as "terrorists" and directed our military forces to eliminate those terrorists? What might happen? His large group of 'dole' supporters might be so forceful to back his dictates that our military forces might have no choice. In the uncertainty and confusion, those people, defending America and our Constitution, would likely be regarded as 'terrorist' and would be annihilated - even by their brothers in the military. Self preservation would be the driving force to make them commit those atrocities - just like the Nazis when they put bullets through innocent peoples' heads and callously exterminated six million Jewish people. Were they evil people, or did they have no choice in order to preserve their own lives?

God bless America, and protect us from Obama and his Muslim forces.

81

Never Forget Benghazi

Remember Benghazi. Why will I not let the Benghazi event die, like the Obama administration is trying to do? With all the lies, deceptions, distractions, and avoidances, Obama hopes Americans will forget about Benghazi. Barack Obama and Hillary Clinton have never given any answer, that's any answer, about the Benghazi event.

Obama said it was caused by a bad video. Hillary pressed the issue that it was caused by a bad video. Obama totally embarrassed Susan Rice by sending her to multiple programs claiming the Benghazi slaughter was caused by a bad video. They all knew they were lying, yet they thought the American public was so stupid they would believe them. Many did; many still do. I don't know about you, but as for me I become insulted when a politician - especially a politician - calls me stupid. I can accept it when a good friend calls me stupid - but not a politician who has absolutely no concept of honesty and honor.

Honesty, honor, duty, and country are the concepts in question regarding the Benghazi event. Four dedicated and brave Americans lost their lives in Benghazi waiting for America to be America; to do what's right; to do everything that's right for an American; to demonstrate the pride, confidence, rightness, and bravery upon which America was founded. The American standard was set long ago.

What would have happened if George Washington's troops had said, "There are too many of them; we don't have a chance to defeat them; we don't want to get involved; we might lose?" On the night they crossed the river, many shoeless and freezing, what would have happened if they had said, "It's too cold?"

Barack Obama and Hillary Clinton didn't say anything except, "It was reaction to a bad video." Their actions indicate they silently said other things; things such as, "We might not get there in time, we might offend the Libyan government, it might be too dangerous, citizens might learn what we were hiding there, it might show the weakness in our leadership." Or perhaps Obama and Hillary didn't consider it an important event. Obama said that was just a, "little bump in the road." Hillary said, "What difference does it make?"

Neither of their comments or actions reflect the character of Americans or America. They have turned their backs on what America is, American foundations and traditions, and what America stands for. With their actions, and lack of American actions, they have discredited America. Their response to the

Benghazi event should be considered a disgrace and reprehensible by every American. As a retired service member, I consider it the gravest insult to every military member who has ever served our great nation and their families who sacrificed along with them.

God bless America - and God protect us from those who would destroy our great traditions and culture.

82

The Saul Alinsky Surprise
12 Rules

Beginning in the 2008 presidential campaign, I noticed something different in Democratic campaigning style and rhetoric. It was subtle, at first, and seemed a bit strange. I wondered why Obama and his supporters were becoming so harsh and 'pushy' in their commentaries, debates, and conversations with talk-show hosts. And, I wondered why they were never 'called out' for all their harshness.

Then, beginning in the 2012 campaign season, everything was clear and predictable. Obama and his supporters, even people not directly connected to the campaign, such as editorial writers and 'letter to the editor' writers, were using the same tactics: attack and disregard the important issues being discussed or questioned.

I also wondered why those on the conservative side were not responding in kind. Only since I've been researching for the 'King Obama' book do I understand why.

It's been well-known that Barack Obama and his close allies have been well-versed and indoctrinated in the 'Saul Alinsky' method. While Obama was connected with the Gamaliel Organization, he attended the Alinsky training school for several weeks - then he taught it during part of his community organizing activities. Obviously, his supporters have taken a cue from their activities and responses - or they have been introduced to the Saul Alinsky techniques themselves. On recently learning this information, I realized I should share it with as many people as possible - so everyone on both sides of these political issues would understand what the overly-aggressive Democrats are doing. They are following the guidelines of Saul Alinsky. It's a concept of: attack, distract, surprise, and confuse the other party.

Bestofluck.com describes Saul Alinsky's '12 Rules for Radicals.' They are:

RULE 1: "Power is not only what you have, but what the enemy thinks you have." Power is derived from 2 main sources – money and people. Have-Nots must build power from flesh and blood. (These are two things of which there is a plentiful supply. Government and corporations always have a difficult time appealing to people, and usually do so almost exclusively with economic arguments.)

RULE 2: "Never go outside the expertise of your people." It results in confusion, fear and retreat. Feeling secure adds to the backbone of anyone. (Organizations under attack wonder why radicals don't address the "real" issues. This is why. They avoid things with which they have no knowledge.)

RULE 3: "Whenever possible, go outside the expertise of the enemy." Look for ways to increase insecurity, anxiety and uncertainty. (This happens all the time. Watch how many organizations under attack are blind-sided by seemingly irrelevant arguments that they are then forced to address.)

RULE 4: "Make the enemy live up to its own book of rules." If the rule is that every letter gets a reply, send 30,000 letters. You can kill them with this because no one can possibly obey all of their own rules. (This is a serious rule. The besieged entity's very credibility and reputation is at stake, because if activists catch it lying or not living up to its commitments, they can continue to chip away at the damage.)

RULE 5: "Ridicule is man's most potent weapon." There is no defense. It's irrational. It's infuriating. It also works as a key pressure point to force the enemy into concessions. (Pretty crude, rude and mean, huh? They want to create anger and fear.)

RULE 6: "A good tactic is one your people enjoy." They'll keep doing it without urging and come back to do more. They're doing their thing, and will even suggest better ones. (Radical activists, in this sense, are no different than any other human being. We all avoid "un-fun" activities, and but we revel at and enjoy the ones that work and bring results.)

RULE 7: "A tactic that drags on too long becomes a drag." Don't become old news. (Even radical activists get bored. So to keep them excited and involved, organizers are constantly coming up with new tactics.)

RULE 8: "Keep the pressure on. Never let up." Keep trying new things to keep the opposition off balance. As the opposition masters one approach, hit them from the flank with something new. (Attack, attack, attack from all sides, never giving the reeling organization a chance to rest, regroup, recover and re-strategize.)

RULE 9: "The threat is usually more terrifying than the thing itself." Imagination and ego can dream up many more consequences than any activist. (Perception is reality. Large organizations always prepare a worst-case scenario, something that may be furthest from the activists' minds. The upshot is that the organization will expend enormous time and energy, creating in its own collective mind the direst of conclusions. The possibilities can easily poison the mind and result in demoralization.)

RULE 10: "If you push a negative hard enough, it will push through and become a positive." Violence from the other side can win the public to your side because the public sympathizes with the underdog. (Unions used this tactic. Peaceful [albeit loud] demonstrations during the heyday of unions in the early to mid-20th Century incurred management's wrath, often in the form of violence that eventually brought public sympathy to their side.)

RULE 11: "The price of a successful attack is a constructive alternative." Never let the enemy score points because you're caught without a solution to the problem. (Old saw: If you're not part of the solution, you're part of the problem. Activist organizations have an agenda, and their strategy is to hold a place at the table, to be given a forum to wield their power. So, they have to have a compromise solution.)

RULE 12: Pick the target, freeze it, personalize it, and polarize it." Cut off the support network and isolate the target from sympathy. Go after people and not institutions; people hurt faster than institutions. (This is cruel, but very effective. Direct, personalized criticism and ridicule works.)

To understand how Obama and Harry Reid are using these tactics, and why they are so effective, just listen to their words as they speak them. Then associate those surprise, aggressive, attack, and far-out charges to these 12 rules. Clearly, the Republicans have never gone to that Saul Alinsky school. If they had, they would be using those same charges of: terrorists and hostage takers. The next time you hear Obama speak, listen closely to his highly-charged words.

God bless America.

83

Ignoring George Bush

Obama and his 'let's blame somebody else' crowd of true American patriots haven't blamed George Bush for anything lately. How can they so quickly forget their number one excuse for all their mishaps, screw-ups, and downright un-American actions? Perhaps those dirty, evil, unpatriotic, uncooperative, terrorist, hostage-taking Republicans in Congress are now a bigger target than Bush. At least at this time they are more convenient.

But, since Obama and his administration refuse to take any responsibility for any of their actions, I believe they should continue to blame George Bush for everything that's gone wrong. After all, isn't Bush the historical leader of all their problems? After only five short years, they shouldn't let Bush off the hook that soon - especially since all their ideas, plans, and activities are so patriotic and perfect, and Bush doesn't let them succeed.

Obama and his patriotic group of American lovers forgot that Bush caused the debacle in 'Operation Fast and Furious.' Bush should have been there to oversee every detail of the operation. He should have known that to track a gunrunning operation, those large weapons should have had miniature tracking devices (in the stocks) that could have been followed by satellites. But, since Bush was too stupid to personally oversee that operation, many military-style weapons fell into the hands of drug cartels. Many are probably also in the hands of terrorists now training in Argentina and Brazil to cross the border one day. Why would Bush arm those terrorists-in-waiting?

And, we can never forget Benghazi. It was George Bush's idea to send those four brave Americans into Benghazi to be slaughtered; and he never said why they were there, why they didn't have sufficient security after they requested it several times, and why they never received any help from American forces who were on standby, and eager, to go to their rescue. Did George Bush advise Obama just to let the drama play out by itself? Bush must have told Obama that his fund-raising trip the next day to Las Vegas was more important. Bush must have forgotten to call Hillary to tell her what to do. Perhaps he couldn't find her; nobody else knows where she was or what she was doing - not even Hillary, herself. Anyway, Bush was responsible for not trying to rescue those four brave men. (Hillary recently said she is finding a new life. Perhaps she was finding a new life with Bill that night, and was too busy to worry about those men in Benghazi.)

I will describe more 'It's Bush's Faults' later. These will include: The IRS scandal, unconstitutional invasion of privacy, and the silent invasion of the Muslim Brotherhood to take over America, and the coming drone invasion. Certainly, Obama and his forces of progressive ideas and opinions have nothing to do with these things foreign to American values and traditions. It has to be George Bush's fault.

God bless America.

84

Clinging To the Office

In my two recent books, and in many of my current blogs, I have proposed the possibility that Barack Obama will never leave office, voluntarily according to our constitution, at the end of his current term. One of the most probable scenarios is that he will allow a security situation near the end of his term to make his declaration of martial law seem logical and appropriate. Is this even conceivable? Is it possible? Who would support him?

Yes, it is conceivable and it is possible. He is testing the waters with this current government shutdown process. He is testing the waters in two major areas. First, is how much support he will get from the populace. Clearly, he knows by now that most will support him. He absolutely refuses to discuss anything with the opposite political party to bring our government back to financial normalcy - and everyone supports him. He arbitrarily closes parks and memorials - that are open and need no security - just to harass good citizens - and his worshipers and doles continue to support him without question. True or not, I heard this morning that contract chaplains will not be allowed to perform their duties on military bases. Obama is testing the waters in every part of our society.

What are the results? If he decides to stay in office by disregarding the constitution, or by martial law, he will be emboldened to do so by his legions of supporters, who forget we have a constitution. Will the military prevent this coup? Absolutely not. They have already demonstrated they will follow his commands even if they are unconstitutional. May God protect us from ourselves. Remember Benghazi.

God bless America.

85

Freedom Lost In The Name Of Security

This is part of an article published 20 Sept., 2013 by The American Thinker. It explains the new Data Hub and gives one of its weaknesses that threatens Americans' personal and financial security. Only two more components combined with the Data Hub will totally eliminate freedom and security from American citizens. We are fast approaching that time under Barack Obama.

"There is increasing concern in Congress over something called the Federal Data Services Hub. The Data Hub is a comprehensive database of personal information being established by the Department of Health and Human Services (HHS) to implement the federally facilitated health insurance exchanges. The purpose of the Data Hub, according to a June 2013 Government Accountability Office (GAO) report, is to provide "electronic, near real-time access to federal data" and "access to state and third party data sources needed to verify consumer-eligibility information." In these days of secret domestic surveillance by the intelligence community, rogue IRS officials and state tax agencies using private information for political purposes, and police electronically logging every license plate that passes by, the idea of the centralized Data Hub is making lawmakers and citizens nervous.

They certainly should be; the potential for abuse is enormous. The massive, centralized database will include comprehensive personal information such as income and financial data, family size, citizenship and immigration status, incarceration status, social security numbers, and private health information. It will compile dossiers based on information obtained from the IRS, the Department of Homeland Security, the Department of Defense, the Veterans Administration, the Office of Personnel Management, the Social Security Administration, state Medicaid databases, and for some reason the Peace Corps. The Data Hub will provide web-based, one-stop shopping for prying into people's personal affairs.

Not to fear, HHS says, the Data Hub will be completely secure. Really? Secure like all the information that has been made public in the Wikileaks era? These days no government agency can realistically claim that private information will be kept private, especially when it is being made so accessible. Putting everyone's personal information in once place only simplifies the challenge for those looking to hack into the system."

What is the second component of 'Freedom Lost?' That second component is a 'cashless' society. A cashless society will add even more personal information to the Data Hub. For instance, without cash the government can track everything you buy and every where you go. Put gas in your car on a major highway twice and the government will know in which direction you travel. Stop at a hotel; have a meal, and the government will know how many are traveling with you. Look for a quiet place of your own to 'chill out.' That place will no longer exist. Our coming Big Brother will be much greater than that described by George Orwell. And, there's more to come under the indefinite Obama administration.

Drones will be everywhere to check on your activities if any of your other Data Hub information gives the security people an alert that you should be visibly watched on a computer monitor. Of course, Obama lovers and his Doles will say you have nothing to fear under Obama and his policies. To give a clue to the great possibilities of security policies he might decide to enforce, what if he declared that anyone hiding outside a monitored zone would be considered a terrorist? Would his worshipers and Doles support him if he were to dictate more security policies like that? Of course they would. After all, you must worship one who can do no wrong.

(An additional thought: In a cashless society, what if a fingerprint or thumb print were the mark to process computer buy and sell transactions? Revelation, Chapter 13, Verses 16 and 17.)

These concepts form the basis of my book-in-process titled, 'Dark Drones: 2025.'

God bless America.

86

A Good Ending

Well - another distraction from getting further along in my new novel, 'Dark Drones,' but it's one of those good distractions about a good-ending story. This is a story about something that turned out right. It's an event that happened yesterday at the World War II Memorial in Washington.

The Mississippi Gulf Coast sponsors an event called the Honor Flight, where WWII veterans are flown to Washington to view the memorial built in their honor. Most are in their 80s and 90s, and most have never seen the memorial. Each veteran is accompanied by another member, a volunteer, called a guardian. Many of the honored veterans are in wheelchairs, and can't fend well for themselves. This was the sixth Gulf Coast Honor Flight, and was scheduled to be the last. Many of those veterans will never have the opportunity to make another trip . There is a big local event when they leave on the flight, and an even larger event at the airport, to honor them, when they return.

When they arrived at the memorial yesterday morning, it was closed; barricaded with 'do not cross' yellow tape. Approximately 100 veterans from Mississippi and an equal number from Iowa sat is dismay. Then, our local congressman, Stephan Palazzo, cut the tape and turned over the barricades to allow them through. He was assisted by three other congressmen from Texas, Florida, and Alabama. Our local Mississippi Gulf Coast group returned last night with great smiles, and you could see their 'Greatest Generation' hearts shining through their bright smiles, even through all the wrinkles and pockmarks on their faces.

There will be many who will try to make a political statement out of this event, however when something like this happens it rises above the call of a political statement. At this point, it doesn't matter who caused the problem, or why. The thing that really matters is that we are all good Americans and should feel the pride those 'Greatest Generation' heroes felt when they visited that memorial that honored them and their service to our country. Barricades are inappropriate for those heroes who will never have another opportunity to view America's respect for their service.

Many of those courageous veterans will leave us before the end of the year; many more within the next year. How many more opportunities will we have to honor them for the sacrifices they made to keep America free? Do we have the ambition, the strength, the courage, and the will to emulate their sacrifices for our great nation? Thank you, four brave congressmen for doing what's right by challenging the anti-American actions of the Obama administration.

God bless America.

87

Life Experiences Create Perspectives

People often choose sides or take a point of view based on their backgrounds, cultural training, and personal experiences. Such is the case with my strong opinions in favor of the Conservative view of our political and social world. I am totally and fully aware that my views are extreme toward the 'Right,' but that's for a specific purpose and it's based on a strong transition of experiences.

The purpose for my extreme views is not to show weakness in my idealist view that one must first try to do something for himself or herself before asking for something or expecting to get something free from others. I fully and totally believe in sharing one's gifts from God, but I also believe one must DO something to share in this same benevolent world in which we live. I believe that concept must be expressed clearly without any room for excuses and wavering. Anyone who wants something for offering no effort to get it will take advantage of any opening or weakness. Laziness and lack of initiative and understanding knows no limits.

The first chapter of my book, 'King Obama: America's Greatest Danger,' introduces this concept. The short introduction explains the dangers we face under our current regime. Then, I use chapter 1 to demonstrate that I once had a different view. In 1955, as a teenager, following a mule plowing a three-acre cotton patch in central Mississippi (seriously- not a joke) I wondered why some people had so much and we had so little. I wondered why those who had more didn't share more. I knew I would never have anything and would always be a failure. Poverty had always reigned throughout my family's history. It wasn't fair. I felt the government should make everything more equal. In my heart I was a Democrat. Thank God, my life experiences changed.

Chapter 1of this book explains that transition that led me to a different perspective and a much better life than I could ever have imagined. This link is a free PDF download here at AD of that chapter. Enjoy.

http://www.authorsden.com/adstorage/1496/King-Chapter-1.pdf

God bless America.

88

Too Important To Ever Forget

I have posted similar comments here before, but they are so important to the history, security, morality, and traditions of our country that they should never be forgotten. They should be reviewed and exposed often. This is a repeat, with added comments, and I plan to repeat this information in some form every month until we have true answers. This question is about Benghazi.

BENGHAZI

Why were four Americans killed there? Recent information suggests the Obama administration was trying to establish an embassy there to demonstrate the 'terrorists' had been defeated. Obama still does not acknowledge his radical Islamist friends as 'terrorists.' Perhaps he considers them 'misguided youth' whom he can redeem with his charming rhetoric. He did make a comment during his first campaign that perhaps with him as president, 'there can be a better understanding.' Perhaps he does not understand 'simplespeak.' Their spoken and written goal is to destroy us - behead us - or make us all Muslim. What part of that does he not understand? (Simplespeak is a term in George Orwell's book, '1984.')

Where was Hillary Clinton while it was happening? Was she hiding in a closet afraid to come out because it might interfere with her ambitions to run for president in 2016? What about that early morning phone call she touted - that she could handle? If she does not have enough courage to say where she was, or what she was doing - does she have enough courage to be a 'Commander-in-Chief? But, as she says, "What difference does it make" when or why four brave Americans were killed. What a display of leadership and true patriotism!

Where was Barack Obama while four brave Americans were being slaughtered in Benghazi? Any real leader would have been there - second by second - trying to save American lives. Even you or I, as regular Americans, would have been there hoping and praying and doing all we could to save those men, as we knew they were being slaughtered. (Did you see those horrible pictures of how the Ambassador was being horribly abused?) Neither you nor I would have allowed that to happen without trying to help. Where was Barack Obama? Was he even involved? His current chief of staff, Denis McDonough, said Obama was 'updated throughout the night.' Leon Panetta, the secretary of defense at that time, said he spoke to the president only once - when the incident began. Why the great deception? Where was Barack Obama (during that phone call Hillary mentioned) throughout the night? Obama has never said - and no reporter has ever had the courage to ask him. He was preparing for his fund-raising trip to Las Vegas the next day - which he proudly attended?

What would you or I have done? We would have called the Libyan leader and said, "Terrorists are attacking Americans on American soil in Libya. Stop this slaughter immediately. American force is on the way to assist you. We will not turn around."

Why did they lie and blame the event on a video? Everyone in the Obama administration blatantly lied about the event. Even Susan Rice went to every news program to proclaim the 'bad' video caused the attack. They all knew it was a lie, but refused to acknowledge the truth. If a president proposes such a blatant and out-front lie as about Benghazi, can that president, and his administration, be trusted on any other occasion? Do they think regular Americans are that stupid? If we accept those lies without question - are we then really that stupid and that unconcerned for the future of our great nation? Then, when Obama finally had to acknowledge the event was not caused by response to the 'bad' video, he called the Benghazi event a 'bump in the road.' (Regardless what caused the Benghazi event, video or otherwise, it was still an event that required action. Obama and his administration failed to take any action.)

Americans are good people. America is a great nation. Although Putin suggests otherwise, America is special. And, since we are special - one nation under God - we must never forget that. We must find answers when evil has been accepted without question.

God bless America

89

The Enemy of Our Enemy

I watched the FOX News interview with Syria's president Assad last night. Clearly, many things he said were falsehoods, or extreme stretches of near truths, however one thing he said touched a little button in the back of my mind regarding our own situation here in the United States. It gets complicated - as does everything in that part of the world. The biggest questions being: who is the real enemy; who is America's real enemy; who should we support; who should we attack? Obama refuses to make these points clear, which puts our country in greater danger. He allows uncertainty to reign in our policies. Confusion does not allow a clear policy for us to follow. For example, he draws red lines that he does not draw.

Perhaps George Bush the First saw the danger many didn't see. When the United States had Iraq's forces on the run from Kuwait, many wondered why Bush didn't allow our military to continue on and destroy Sadam Hussein's regime. At that time it would have been easy. I also wondered that at the same time. Now, I realize that Sadam's regime was one of the props in the balance of power in that region. If he had been removed, the radical Islamists - especially from Iran - would certainly have started their activity sooner. George Bush the Second made that big blunder. He removed Sadam and that opened Pandora's box in that region. Now everything is so hodge-podge and screwed up in that part of the world that no one knows whom to support, or whom to oppose.

Obama's idea was to throw a few Tomahawk missiles into Syria to 'teach Assad a lesson.' He said the idea was not to remove Assad from power. What kind of policy is that? What if those missiles Obama was so anxious to shoot into Syria had killed more innocent civilians than did the gas Assad supposedly used. Would that have made Americans 'war criminals?' (Remember: Obama said he did not draw the red line - America drew the red line.) Would that have endeared us to the innocent Syrian people? We have not declared war on Syria. Syria has not attacked the Untied States. What lesson would that really be? And, that doesn't address the main issue - that Obama disregards or ignores: who is America's true enemy? If Obama were truthful and honorable he would say our enemy is the same enemy of Syria, Iraq, Afghanistan, Libya, Egypt and the rest of the Muslim world under attack by Radical Islamists. Our common enemy is the radical Islamic jihadists.

Perhaps we will face that common enemy one day in America -

confused with patriots proclaimed to be 'terrorists.' Why did the DHS describe some returning veterans as a possible threat against our government - by being influenced by anti-government groups? Why is our government procuring domestic military armored vehicles? Why has our government bought 1.6 billion rounds of military ammunition - almost half a million rounds of that being hollow-point bullets? Hollow-points are designed to destroy and kill - not for target practice.

Who is their enemy? Who is our enemy? What is America's guiding policy against any enemy? Perhaps the answer is that Obama will draw more red lines - that someone else will be accused of drawing.

God bless America.

90

Somewhere and Sometime

After writing two chapters of my planned novel, 'Escape from Troy,' I decided to put that one on hold awhile and write one that's more current and relevant. I just finished two chapters (10,000 words) this week on a new one tentatively titled, 'Dark Drones.' Or maybe I will title it, '2025' after Orwell's novel, '1984.' Anyway, this excerpt is a sample of how I plan to relate current events (under Barack Obama), including biblical relationships, into a dark novel.

To set the stage, this is a group of survivalists preparing for the future. Three of their members were mysteriously killed with beams of light from the sky as they were entering their safe zone. Carl was targeted when he purchased a shovel at the hardware store, and that purchase created an alert at the security monitoring center. Carl is now using the shovel in his back yard to reduce suspicion. Evelyn is his wife.Richard and Marty are visiting them during the evening. The excerpt begins:

"Richard continued, "Power created is power unleashed and uncontrolled. The government has created power beyond its human inhibitions; they will never stop until they exercise all they have." He listened to the quietness a moment then explained that the government has become like the leader of a wild animal pack - a pride of lions. The leader knows he's in total control until his power becomes diminished by someone stronger. He doesn't voluntarily give up that total control. "These leaders in the government are like that lion king; they don't know when to draw the limit; no conscience of sharing."

"Maybe our government really is like that lion king. He pretends to protect the pride, but what he's really doing is focusing on his own power, influence, and selfish needs - that uncontrolled drive for total power," Carl added.

"I guess you're right," Evelyn agreed. "When a lion takes over a pride, the first thing he does is kill all the young ones so he gets more of what he wants. Males or females, it doesn't matter; he just kills them to start his own - to get what he wants, not what the group needs."

Marty said that's probably what happened to Jack, Robert, and Martin when they were struck down out of the clear blue sky. He added that obviously they were seen as a threat to the establishment and were killed, just like those young lions. They were seen as a threat, and were discarded like some kind of useless trash.

"Speaking of the clear blue sky, that reminds me of something I saw today," Carl said. "While I was working in the yard, I saw an oblong blue spot in the sky. It was blue for awhile when the white clouds passed behind it. Then it turned white like the clouds until the clouds passed; then it faded to the sky blue again and I lost sight of it." He paused then added, "It was strange; don't think I was imagining it."

Evelyn said, "I told him it looked like a little hole in the cloud. But, I didn't have time to look close. I was in a hurry."

"The sky was blue, clear blue, when our three men were stuck down," Richard exclaimed. "I wonder if there's a connection."

"We didn't see anything," Marty agreed, "just some quick flashes from the sky, then Jack, Robert, and Martin were down on the ground - didn't move a muscle after they were hit." Then he asked Carl if he had seen anything else, such as flashes of light.

"No, just that oblong thing up in the sky. I couldn't even tell how far away it was. It could have been directly over my head, or up in the clouds. There was nothing to create a good perspective."

Richard said he had mentioned that event to his pastor after it happened, during Jack's funeral. He added that the pastor didn't want to talk about it much, but he did mention something about the beast demonstrating miracles by bringing fire down from the sky. "He recited something about Revelation and Chapter Thirteen, but said not to talk about it. He said folks wouldn't believe you and would call you crazy, anyway."

"Well, for whatever reason, somebody's watching us. I saw that thing in the sky, and even before that, I saw the car that followed me home from the hardware store. They must be connected." Carl added that nobody had contacted him or had been seen observing him since the day of the event at the store.

Evelyn said she had been shopping for some of their needed items, and had never had the feeling she was being followed or observed. She also said none of the other people helping her collect those items had mentioned being questioned or followed. She concluded, "Maybe things aren't as severe as they seem on the surface."

"Perhaps not," Marty replied. "But, we got lots to do, and just one little mistake might cause the deaths of all of us - in the name of security by our government." End of excerpt.

I hope to have this finished by January, my next birthday. I'll be 75. After that, folks might start calling me a 'doodling old man.' Or, did that start last year? I can't remember.

God bless America.

91

Anti-Leadership Leadership

A serious, but ignored threat to the economic prosperity of America is the school dropout rate. It's now approaching 25 percent, and would be higher if, in many cases, certificates were not substituted for diplomas. The problem: students are being brainwashed with social ideas, not taught how to learn. Isn't it ironical that teachers spend many years in school learning their subject matter and learning how to teach, but students are never given simple instructions on how to receive and process that instruction - how to learn?

Even worse, our government has no real interest in improving education effectiveness in America. Two things immediately prove this point. First, the worst education leader in America, Arne Duncan, was appointed as the Secretary of Education. He was head of the Chicago school system before his appointment. He was selected from the most failing school system in America to lead American students. Why?

Secondly, social and Islamic courses are being substituted for real education: reading, writing, and arithmetic. I just heard on news this morning that the United States now ranks 35th in Math, and 35th overall, in education effectiveness. Would a leader really want a less-educated society? Consider the possibilities. Lack of inspiration in schools is one of the greatest incentives for students to drop out. If they aren't learning what they need, why should they stay there?

A high dropout rate not only jeopardizes our national prosperity and opportunity, it also has two other specific and critical results. Most, almost all, prisoners are high school dropouts. Most people on public welfare are high school dropouts. The dropout rate is compounded when people on welfare have more children, and don't know how to help them read, study, and learn. Can you imagine what prosperity would be gained, or how much taxes could be lowered if the dropout rate could simply be reduced to half its current rate?

My book, 'Student Study Skills,' is a condensed version of my book, 'How To Learn.' It has a short story explaining how learning is a step-by-step process, ten parent assistance ideas, twenty specific study skills, and short, condensed study skills for younger students.

The key to education success in America is direct parental involvement and support. Our government tries to convince people otherwise - that the government will take care of it by making the school system better with more taxpayer money, and by making teachers more accountable. Education always begins at home.

Here, I am offering a free book to help those weak parents, and weak students, learn how to fulfill their responsibilities. The book is titled, 'Student Study Skills.' It's free. You can download it here at Smashwords under the name 'Positive Learning Skills, copy it, and distribute it all you want. Even if you remove my list of other books on the last page - I don't care. Download this book, give it to someone, and help someone learn - so they can help us save our great nation. It's an individual thing, since our government is now useless, or even a negative factor in the success of our nation.

92

A Message for Help

Dear Facebook friends: I am asking you to help me present a strong Conservative and patriotic American point of view and a lesson to our Liberal friends and Obama lovers. Tomorrow is the anniversary of the Benghazi disaster, where Obama and his administration failed our great nation, and then used excuses and denials to cover up what really happened. Four brave Americans were mercilessly slaughtered, and everyone connected with Obama denies, distracts, and refuses to explain why these brave men died - without any hope of assistance or rescue. It was an action, or inaction, never experienced on any battlefield during the long history of the United States. Americans always try to help other Americans when they are in peril. Obama and his administration refused to help, and then covered up their atrocity. Their un-American actions must never be forgotten.

What can you do to make our feelings known? Tomorrow, at 6:00 a.m. I will post the following article at my blog site at Authorsden. Then, I will post the link to the blog on my timeline. Every time you click on the link, it records a 'like' at the blog site. It does not identify you or your address. It just automatically records a 'like.' If you agree with the article below, please click on the link when I post it in the morning. You can even do it more than once. It will drive the Liberals and Obama lovers crazy if they see 50 to 100 likes. The most I have had, so far, is 15. Please share this if you agree with the article and would like to help show the Obama administration how real Americans feel. Thanks for your participation:

The Benhgazi Disaster.

On Dec.7, 1941, we know what happened at Pearl Harbor and who was responsible, and why. We were Americans - and came together as one. On Sept. 11, 2001, we know what happened, who was responsible, and why. We were Americans - and came together as one. On Sept. 11, 2012 - one year ago today - something bad happened to four brave Americans in Benghazi, Libya. It was another attack on America. But on this occasion Obama and his administration thrust doubt and secrets into America's heart and soul. They refused, and still refuse, to give Americans enough information to understand the radical Islamic enemy. Obama denies Americans the opportunity to come together as one.

Or is it just the radical Islamists? Who should we fear most - the radical Islamists, or our government who is becoming more and more deceitful and dishonest? Real American idealism is founded upon and based on truth and honesty. Obama and his administration are stripping Americans of that foundation - in every word they utter.

Obama has never explained why four brave Americans were slaughtered in Benghazi. He only claimed it was the result from the response to a video, and was only a little "bump in the road." Hillary Clinton has never explained why those four brave Americans died serving our great nation - under her direct supervision. She also blamed that video then said, "What difference does it make?" Susan Rice vehemently claimed those four died because of a video - not from a planned terrorist attack. For her deceptive support to the president, she was rewarded with a job promotion.

I watched a video, yesterday, where Denis McDonough, Obama's current Chief of Staff, was on Face the Nation, on Feb. 17, 2013. Listening to his comments reminded me of two rules taught by Saul Alinsky. They are rule 5: Ridicule is man's most potent weapon, and rule 12: The price of a successful attack is a constructive alternative. These four people used Alinsky's rules to deny, distract, and say something so absurd that those new comments would become the focus of the conversation - so the truth about the original topic could be avoided.

McDonough said Obama was updated throughout the night of the Benghazi event. Leon Panctta said the president was called once. In reality, Obama was preparing for his fund-raising trip to Las Vegas the next day and didn't have time to worry about Americans being slaughtered in Benghazi.

Then McDonough said, "We worked this throughout the night - the secretary of defense and the chairman of the JCS." McDonough was the deputy national security advisor at that time.

Then he said, "President Obama did not call the Libyan president -

Hillary Clinton called on his behalf." (Remember - Hillary Clinton said she did not know what was happening. She said only, "What difference does it make."

Finally, McDonough used the classic Alinsky attack. He chastised the interviewer for bringing up ancient history, and boastfully proclaimed that Obama has taken bold action to make sure something like this never happens again. He distracted and attacked - just like the Saul Alinsky rules describe.

http://www.cbsnews.com/video/watch/?id=50141223n

What can be done to counter this Alinsky agenda? Interviewers and Conservatives must be aware that it will be used against them - and be prepared to throw it back on Obama and his minions twice as hard.

God bless America.

93

They Can't Be Serious

Since I've been researching and writing about Obama's close relationship and support of Islamic radicals, a major question remains deep in my mind regarding his strongest supporters. First, he never criticizes Islamic radicals or calls them terrorists.

Secondly, he has six of them formally in his administration who are open supporters of the Muslim Brotherhood. The Brotherhood is strong proponents of Sharia law. Sharia law requires the harshest actions against Obama's strong supporters: women and homosexuals. What does Sharia say should happen to women and homosexuals?

I have reported this full list before in a blog, and in my books, but these are the laws specific to Obama's strongest supporters. This is from an article titled, 'Islamic Law in Brief!,' written February 4, 2011, by Syed Kamran Mirza. He states, "These common laws of 'Islamic Sharia' which are regularly practiced in the Islamically ruled (Sharia-based) nations with some minor variations:

17. No testimony in court is acceptable from people of low-level jobs, such as street sweepers or a bathhouse attendant. Women in such low level jobs such as professional funeral mourners cannot keep custody of their children in case of divorce.

19. Homosexuality is punishable by death.

20. There is no age limit for marriage of girls under Sharia. The marriage contract can take place anytime after birth and consummated at age 8 or 9.

21. Rebelliousness on the part of the wife nullifies the husband's obligation to support her, gives him permission to beat her and keep her from leaving the home.

22. Divorce is only in the hands of the husband and is as easy as

saying: "I divorce you" and becomes effective even if the husband did not intend it.

23. There is no common property between husband and wife and the husband's property does not automatically go to the wife after his death.

24. A woman inherits half what a man inherits. Sister gets half of what brother gets.

25. A man has the right to have up to 4 wives and wife has no right to divorce him even if he is polygamous.

26. The dowry is given in exchange for the woman's sexual organs.

27. A man is allowed to have sex with slave women and also with women captured in battle (concubines), and if the enslaved woman is married her marriage is annulled.

28. The testimony of a woman in court is half the value of a man; that is, two women equal to one man.

29. A woman loses custody if she remarries.

30. A rapist may only be required to pay the bride-money (dowry) without marrying the rape victim.

31. A Muslim woman must cover every inch of her body which is considered "Awrah," a sexual organ. Some schools of Sharia allow the face and some don't.

32. A Muslim man is forgiven if he kills his wife caught in the act of adultery. However, the opposite is not true for women since he "could be married to the woman he was caught with."

34. The perpetrators of genocide, mass rape and plunder will not be punished if they repent.

35. To prove rape, a woman must have 4 male witnesses. Women's testimony is not accepted - Pakistan's Hudood ordnance 7 of 1979 amended by 8B of 1980. Thousands of raped women and girls in many countries have been charged with Zena (physical relations outside marriage) and punished by Sharia courts for want of witnesses.

So, with all these rules in Sharia Law, what does Islam say about truth and honesty? It's required that Muslims defend Islam, even if they must be dishonest. In Mirza's article he emphasizes, "Caution! Islam permits devout Muslims to lie, cheat, and deliberately bluff non-Muslims to protect or promote his religion of Islam, anytime, anywhere. And this tactic is known as "Islamic Taqiyya" and was originally used by the Prophet of Islam to fool, and later subjugate and destroy enemies of Islam. As Prophet of Islam repeatedly asserted: "War is a deception" and with this holy-tactic, Prophet of Islam established his most intolerant religion of violence (by 80 plus bloody battles) which he later named as: 'religion of peace'!"

He continues, "Therefore, today's Islamists will follow the holy path of their Prophet and will deny that—Sharia is really Islamic law! They will try to cheat by saying that, all these Sharia laws that are practiced in Saudi Arabia, Iran, Sudan, and elsewhere are not true Islamic, and they have been distorted."

My question is: why is Obama supporting and promoting those who would create the harshest conditions against his strongest backers and supporters? Perhaps they should consider the concept of 'Taqiyya' described above before giving Obama their full allegiance.

God bless America.

94

The Balance Of Power

Isn't it amazing how one little comment can change one's plans for the day? This morning, I got up at 5:00, as usual, had my bowl of cereal (Raisin bran mixed with Honey Bunches of Oats) then went outside and got the newspaper for my wife when she gets up. Then I planned to work on a new novel, tentatively titled: 'Dark Drones.' It's more current than the one I was working on: 'From Troy to Ephesus.' Troy has been around a long time - waiting a little longer shouldn't matter.

While I do my light work on my computer, I listen to news in the background. When I get deeper into a book, I listen to quiet music. While I was doing light work, I heard Obama say, "There will be no boots on the ground in Syria." I looked at the TV and saw his face filling the whole screen. It instantly reminded me of when he said, "If you like your health care plan, you can keep your health care plan. If you like your doctor, you can keep your doctor." I also wondered if it's less painful to die when half your cranium is blown off by shrapnel than to die by chemical weapons. Or, when Islamic radicals tie your hands behind your back, make you kneel with your face down, then put two large bullets through your brain - as shown in a recent article.

Obama's face filled the screen when he uttered those falsehoods at that time. Even his expression during those comments spewed deceit. Perhaps at this time, he believes what he says, also perhaps he has not considered all the possible consequences of allowing Islamic rebels to take over Syria. If he weakens the present Syrian government, what's likely to happen? It could eventually lead to a biblical event. Eliminating Sadam Hussein in Iraq began the destruction of the balance of power in the Middle East. Attacking Syria could take it even a step further.

If the Syrian government is toppled by the Islamic rebels, what will happen to their vast stockpile of chemical weapons? Will those radical Islamists be prudent and fair, and eliminate them or turn them over to the United Nations? Or will they deliver them with missiles and suicide bombers into Israel? (Could that be the rider of the 'Pale Horse?') If the radical Islamists take over Syria, who will be next? Will it be Jordan and Turkey, and other countries that are now somewhat moderate in their world view? Will that allow the Muslim Brotherhood another foot in the door for spreading their plan for world domination? They intend to destroy us and the entire Western world. It's in their written charter, and it's taught as their way of life and their destiny. Why is Obama so intent on helping them achieve that goal?

Okay, back to that novel - what was the title? I've got to get this finished in time for golf this afternoon. Was it Troy, or Ephesus?

God bless America.

95

Believable Threats

There's a news report this morning that Iran threatens retaliation against the United States if Obama attacks Syria. Of course, the Syrian government also says they will retaliate. Are their threats credible - and how could they be carried out?

I've been researching this question at least two years to write about Obama's relationship with Islamists. There are several possible scenarios of how their threats could be carried out, but here I will offer just one consideration. This scenario also considers the idea that Obama will not give up his leadership position at the end of his elected term. Consider this information and its relationship to positioning for future total control. I won't spell it out in detail - it's too unbelievable. Consider it for yourself.

Atlanta's WSB-TV2 station published a population breakdown from an Immigration and Customs Enforcement staging facility in Florence, Arizona., dated April 15, 2010, which includes detainees from as far away as Afghanistan, Armenia, Bosnia, Egypt, Ghana, Iraq, Iran, Jordan, Kenya, Morocco, Pakistan, Sudan, Uzbekistan, Yemen, Botswana, Turkey, and many other countries. Based on U.S. Border Patrol statistics, there were 30,147 other than Mexicans (OTM) apprehended in fiscal year 2003; 44, 614 in fiscal year 2004; 165,178 in fiscal year 2005; and 108,025 in fiscal year 2006. Most were caught along the U.S. Southwest border.

That report added, "U.S. Immigration and Customs Enforcement investigations have revealed that aliens were smuggled from the Middle East to staging areas in Central and South America, before being smuggled illegally into the United States. Members of Hezbollah have already entered the United States across the Southwest border. U.S. military and intelligence officials believe that Venezuela is emerging as a potential hub of terrorism in the Western Hemisphere. The Venezuelan government is issuing identity documents that could subsequently be used to obtain a U.S. visa and enter the country." Former U.S. Representative J.D. Hayworth concluded, "We have left the back door to the United States open. We have to understand that there are definitely people who mean to do us harm who have crossed that border."

A more recent report, June 8, 2013 by Kirstin Tate of mrconservative.com confirmed that information, and added:

"It is usually assumed that most illegals caught crossing the US/Mexican border are South Americans. You may be surprised to learn, however, that thousands of the illegals caught crossing the borders are classified as "OTMs" (Other Than Mexicans). A substantial number of these OTMs are Muslim terrorists. Records from a detention center near Phoenix, AZ, show illegals from Afghanistan, Egypt, Iran, Iraq, Pakistan, Sudan, and Yemen in custody."

What would happen if these terrorists sneaking into the United States, from southern borders or anywhere else, became active near the end of Obama's current term? Is there any better excuse for a president, especially Barack Obama, to declare martial law - and never let go? Is it even conceivable that a real United States president could consider such a tyrannical action? What if this activity began before the end of his term?

Where are those weapons lost during 'Fast and Furious' and other 'gunrunning' operations? Why has the Obama government bought 1.6 billion rounds of ammunition - including half a million rounds of hollow point bullets? They refuse to give an answer. Why does Obama refuse to criticize Islamic terrorists, or even call them Islamic terrorists - even when they slaughter our American brothers in Benghazi? Why are three of his senior advisors so anti-American? Why does he have many Muslim Brotherhood supporters in his advisory administration?

Who is Barack Obama, and what are his plans for America?

God bless America.

96

Truths and Half-Truths

Yesterday, Russian president Vladimir Putin called John Kerry a 'liar' regarding his testimony about the Syrian situation and use of chemical weapons - gas. Certainly, our first inclination is to conclude it's just a typical Russian response to support one of their friends and allies. But, in this crazy world of political rhetoric and propaganda to support an agenda, who knows the real truth - and why such sides are taken?

Even our own tragic 'Civil War' in the 1860s evolved from half-truths and verbal miscalculations - the worst tragedy in American history. And, our great nation is still somewhat divided from that horrendous event. It seems that's normal, for most nations always have some divisive ideals, which explains the differences in political parties. Within either idealism, however, truth should be the guiding light.

I would like to strongly disagree with Putin's assessment of John Kerry's character, but I question the honesty and veracity of both sides. Of course, as Americans we must distrust the 'evil Russians.' Remember that movie, 'The Russians are Coming?' My distrust of John Kerry, however, is more personal. I watched his testimony, on television, before the Senate Committee on Foreign

Relations in 1971, when he testified that American troops in Vietnam:

"...had personally raped, cut off ears, cut off heads, taped wires from portable telephones to human genitals and turned up the power, cut off limbs, blown up bodies, randomly shot at civilians, razed villages in fashion reminiscent of Ghengis Khan, shot cattle and dogs for fun, poisoned food stocks, and generally ravaged the countryside of South Vietnam..." and accused the U.S. military of committing war crimes "on a day-to-day basis with the full awareness of officers at all levels of command."

John Kerry served only four months in Vietnam, in 1968 - 1969. I served a year there in 1966-1967. We were both in our mid-20s. I was four years older than Kerry. Although I was not involved with active combat, I was aware of events taking place - and I knew Americans were serving honorably. I'm sure out of fear or frustration some mistakes were made, but in general our troops would not intentionally do something as horrendous as Kerry claimed. Besides, how could he gain that much deep knowledge in just four months? He was too busy playing Admiral on a River Boat.

As I watched his presentations the past two days, John Kerry expressed the same attitude and demeanor he did during that Senate hearing in 1971. Clearly, he enjoys the lime-light, and having his words heard - whether there is any truth in those words or not. Who can we believe? This is the link to Kerry's 1971 testimony.

http://www.youtube.com/watch?v=ucY7JOfg6G4

God bless America.

97

Obama's Threats

"Okay, Little Bobby, if you do that one more time, I'm going to give you a good spanking." "Okay, Bobby, you do that one more time, I'm going to make you stand in the corner for an hour." "Okay, Bobby, you do that one more time, and you won't get your allowance next week." "Okay, Bobby, you do that again, and you can't play your computer games for a week." "Okay, Bobby, just wait until your daddy gets home."

Does this sound familiar? Doesn't this sound very similar to what our president - the President of the United States of America - is telling the President of Syria? Is this that phone call Hillary Clinton mentioned when she was campaigning against Barack Obama a few years ago? Obama opened his big deceptive mouth the first time with a 'red line' and now he doesn't know how to get out of it, so he's waiting for Congress (Daddy getting home) to take care of it for him. In the meantime, his big talk has made the United States more irrelevant in world affairs and has once again put Israel in greater danger. Why?

He puts Israel in greater danger for three reasons. First, is his personal dislike of Israel and Israel's prime minister. Second, is his appointment of Samantha Power as his Ambassador to the

United Nations. She is strongly anti-Israel, and has even written that Israel should be invaded to make them comply with the needs of the Palestinians. Third, he has many Muslims in his administration who are considered senior advisors. Many of those appointees are also members of the Muslim Brotherhood and the two most prominent Islamic groups that subscribe to a written document that they will make the United States an Islamic country from within.

What is Obama's dilemma in this Syrian question? Likely, it's the question of future votes to support his socialistic and Islamic agenda. It's certainly not what's in the best interests for our great nation - the United States of America, or the survivability of Israel.

God bless America.

98

It's Not 'His' Military

I was watching news at 5:00 this morning, in the background, while going through my usual activity of checking emails, authorsden, and all the other sites we hope will show the sale of another book or two. All of a sudden, in the background, I heard a comment from Obama that distracted me from my computer queries. That comment was, "my military." The comment was so unusual, and out of place, I had to stop and check it out.

Since I couldn't do a replay on TV, I made the query on my computer by inputting 'Obama's comments on Syria.' That brought up a replay of what I had just heard on TV. In discussing his indecision (of which of his dangerous Islamic friends to support) Obama included the following statement:

"I have had my military and our team look at a wide range of options."

Of course I played the video several times to understand the full impact of what he said and the implication. To most, I'm sure the statement was innocuous and of no concern, but when I heard it in the background it certainly made a great impact on my continuing distrust of this man - and my feelings about the security of our country. Is our United States military 'his' military? Of course, he is the commander-in-chief, but our military is not his possession. I doubt if even George Washington ever said, "my military," while he was suffering with them on the battlefield - and shivering with them in freezing weather as they crossed that river to secure 'OUR' freedom.

Our military is 'our' military. It's part of us. It's a thing and concept of honor that most of us cherish. It is not the possession of a president - or any one person. Those of us who served - and there are many of us - understand this concept. With this attitude of Obama's - what dangers lie ahead for our great nation?

God bless America.

99

The Smoking Gun

What is Barack Obama's relationship with the Muslim Brotherhood and radical Islamists who are trying to destroy America and the Western world? Why does he refuse to call Islamic terrorists, 'terrorists?' Perhaps a statement he made in 2007 gives a fundamental clue.

On November 21, 2007, then-candidate Obama said on New Hampshire Public Radio that his Muslim experience would make us safer. He said:

"I truly believe that the day I'm inaugurated, not only the country looks at itself differently, but the world looks at America differently. If I'm reaching out to the Muslim world they understand that I've lived in a Muslim country and I may be a Christian, *but I also understand their point of view.*

My sister is half-Indonesian. I traveled there all the way through my college years. And so I'm intimately concerned with what happens in these countries and the cultures and perspective these folks have. And those are powerful tools for us to be able to reach out to the world. Then I think the world will have confidence that I am listening to them and that our future and our security is tied up with our ability to work with other countries in the world that will ultimately make us safer."

Is Obama delusional, or is he lost in la-la land? The radical Muslim terrorist goal is to destroy us and anyone else who is not or does not convert to Islam. Why does he think his relationship with them, or who he is, will change that dogma? But, he still refuses to criticize them and express who they really are - terrorists. Why? Does he need them for his ultimate aims? Radical includes the Muslim Brotherhood - several members are now in Obama's administration!

The 'Investigative Project on Terrorism' discovered the Islamic conspiratorial plan for the silent Islamic Jihad in America. Clearly and explicitly the proposal, and acceptance by most if not all, of these organizations is to destroy the United States and its religious foundation from WITHIN. What is Barack Obama's reaction to their plan and his attitude toward their approach? He embraces them - in his own words. This is from an interview with Steve Kroft, on 60 Minutes, where Obama made the 'bump in the road' comment after four Americans were murdered in Benghazi, and he refused to blame Islamic radicals. He said:

"Well, I've said even at the time that this is going to be a rocky path. The question presumes that somehow we could have stopped this wave of change. I think it was absolutely the right thing for us to do to align ourselves with democracy, universal rights, a notion that people have to be able to participate in their own governance.

But I was pretty certain and continue to be pretty certain that there are going to be bumps in the road because you know, in a lot of these places the one organizing principle has been Islam, the one part of society that hasn't been controlled completely by the government. There are strains of extremism, and anti-Americanism, and anti-Western sentiment. And you know can be tapped into by demagogues.

There will probably be some times where we bump up against some of these countries and have strong disagreements, but I do think that over the long term, we are more likely to get a Middle East and North Africa that is more peaceful, more prosperous and more aligned with our interests."

What did Obama say? (*"the one organizing principle has been Islam, the one part of society that hasn't been controlled completely by the government."*) Obama's comments fall right in line with that 'Investigative Project' report. **It's the 'smoking gun' that links Obama directly to the Muslim Brotherhood intentions.** He is sending them millions of our honest American dollars - while he wants more American dollars from more 'rich people.' I ask again, "What are this man's intentions?"

God bless and protect America.

About the Author

Will Clark's author experiences began by writing inspection and evaluation reports in the U.S. Air Force. He is a retired Air Force officer and a Vietnam veteran, serving in Saigon from 1966 to 1967. His other overseas assignments include Misawa, Japan and Ankara, Turkey.

In 1995, he authored a book, *How to Learn*, as a county-wide study skills project to encourage students to improve their grades in DeSoto County, Mississippi. Education supporters printed and distributed four thousand copies. He also wrote a weekly education column for a local newspaper, *The Desoto County Tribune,* the following school year.

His next published book was *School Bells and Broken Tales*, a parody of nursery rhyme characters, also a motivation and education book for children. His other books include *Shades of Retribution*, a historical novel, and *Simply Success*, a motivation guide for students and employees.

His action novels include a trilogy based on Atlantis and crystals. The first book is titled: *The Atlantis Crystal.* The second book is titled: *She Waits In Atlantis.* The third is: *Return to Atlantis.* This trilogy is based on his travels while assigned to Turkey, site of the ancient city of Troy.

His previous political action novel, *666: Mark of the Beast*, is a sequel to another political action novel, *America 20XX: The New World Order.*

Clark and his wife, Marie, live in Diamondhead, Mississippi, where they play golf with many friends.

Things We Must Never Forget
Until We Know All the Answers

Benghazi
Why were four Americans killed?
Where was Hillary Clinton while it was happening?
Where was Barack Obama while it was happening?
Why did they lie and blame the event on a video?
Why were rescuers on 'stand by' told to 'stand down?'

Fast and Furious
Who authorized the operation?
Why did the operation continue after weapons were lost?
Why did the procedure have no procedure?
Why weren't tracking devices used?

The IRS Scandal
What was the highest level involved?
Who initiated it?
Why hasn't anyone been fired or reprimanded?

Greatest Quotes
of
Our Time

Michelle Obama
February 18, 2008
"For the first time in my adult life I am proud of my country."
(Age 44)

Barack Obama
March 9, 2008
"We are no longer a Christian nation - at least not just."

Nancy Pelosi
March 9, 2010
"We have to pass the bill so that you can find out what is in it."

Hillary Clinton
January 23, 2013
"What difference, at this point, does it make?"

Other Books by the Author

Novels:
Shades of Retribution
The Atlantis Crystal
She Waits in Atlantis
Return to Atlantis
America 20XX: The New World Order
666: Mark of the Beast
Death Drones: 2025

Childrens' Books:
Forest Trails and Fairy Tales
Wishing Wells and Broken Tales
Student Study Skills
American Heroes: Students Who Learn

Non-Fiction:
Simply Success
The Education Jungle
How to Learn
The Day America Died
Obama's Ring: The Seat of Satan
Managing Without Conflict
The Peer Pressure Monster
Denied 3 Times

www.ingramcontent.com/pod-product-compliance
Lightning Source LLC
Chambersburg PA
CBHW060246290526
45789CB00001B/218